WRITING

Aspirations

Remember to think about

- What has helped me learn effectively today?
- What strategies could I use to progress further?
- In what other subjects could I apply these skills?
- When could I use these skills outside of school?

Badger Publishing

Badger Publishing Limited
15 Wedgwood Gate
Pin Green Industrial Estate
Stevenage, Hertfordshire SG1 4SU
Telephone: 01438 356907   Fax: 01438 747015
www.badger-publishing.co.uk
enquiries@badger-publishing.co.uk

Badger KS3 English
Aspirations • Writing

First published 2009
ISBN 978-1-84691-458-4

Text © Jonathan Morgan 2009
Complete work © Badger Publishing Limited 2009

All rights reserved. No part of this publication may be reproduced, stored in any form or by any other means mechanical, electronic, recording or otherwise without the prior permission of the publisher.

The right of Jonathan Morgan to be identified as author of this work has been asserted by him in accordance with the Copyright, Design and Patents Act 1988.

Acknowledgements
With thanks to the following for permission to reproduce the following copyright materials: British Heart Foundation, NSPCC, Manchester Tourism Board, The Home Office, Parentline Plus, The Independent (newspaper), The Mirror (newspaper), Star Course (website), Helium (website), Bloodaxe, BBC (website), Mark Boardman (website), The Guardian (newspaper), Rotten Tomatoes (website)

Efforts to contact other copyright holders have proved unsuccessful. If any of them would care to contact Badger Publishing Limited, we will be happy to make appropriate arrangements.

Publisher: David Jamieson
Editor: Danny Pearson
Designer: Fiona Grant
Cover Photo: Getty Images

Printed and bound in China through Colorcraft Limited, Hong Kong

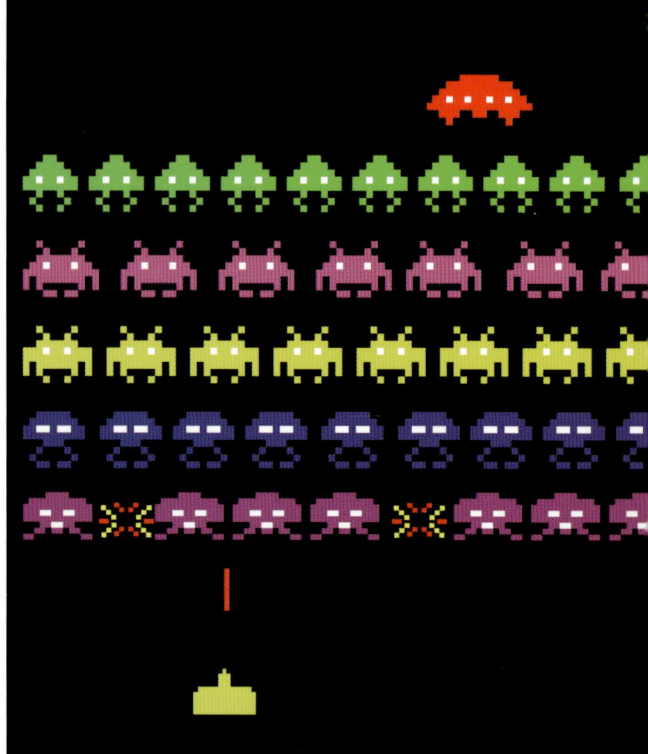

Aspirations — Writing contents

Chapter 1 **Introduction** *Page 3*	Becoming a more creative, engaging and independent writer.	
Chapter 2 **Creative Licence.** *Page 8*	**Prose**	*Holes* - Louis Sachar *Page 20* *Eveline (Dubliners)* - James Joyce *Page 25* *Hard Times* - Charles Dickens *Page 29*
	Poetry	*Timothy Winters* - Charles Causley *Page 32* *What Stephen Lawrence Has Taught Us* - Benjamin Zephaniah *Page 35* *One reply to Euthanasia* - Doris Manning *Page 38* *The Town Frowns on the Country Clown* *Page 40*
	Scriptwriting	*Mourning Glory* (Radio script) *Page 43* *Dracula* (TV script) *Page 44* www.bbc.co.uk/writersroom *No Flies on Me* (film script) *Page 45*
Chapter 3 **This time it's personal.** *Page 60*	**Recount**	*Here's how I quit smoking* *Page 65* www.quitsmokingsupport.com *Unreliable Memoirs* - Clive James' autobiography *Page 71* *Kathryn* - Jillian Morgan's diary entry *Page 75*
	Letter writing	*Mamas & Papas* letter of complaint *Page 82*
	Blogs	*The Yellow Blog Road* - Mark Boardman www.yellowblogroad.com *Page 86*

Aspirations — Writing contents

Chapter 4
Shape it, sort it, write it.
Page 99

Leaflets	HACK anti-smoking leaflet - British Heart Foundation *Page 108*
	Cruelty to children must stop. FULL STOP NSPCC *Page 115*
	Personal Safety - Home Office *Page 122*
	Got a teenager? Parentline Plus *Page 125*
Articles	Scientist lament 40 years of fatal smoking *Page 129*
	Family faces jail for watching cancer victim kill herself (The Independent) *Page 133*
	Drug victim's parent defends death images (The Guardian) *Page 136*
	So close to a real disaster & Derby double for Sven - The Mirror *Pages 140 & 147*
Advertising	Uniquely Manchester – Manchester Tourism Board *Page 148*

Chapter 5
Rights, Candour, Action
Page 159

Speeches	Yes we can! - President Barrack Obama's election victory speech. *Page 168*
	Bill Clinton's apology to the American public *Page 177*
	Charles Spencer's tribute to Princess Diana *Page 182*
Commentary	Non-religious arguments against voluntary euthanasia *Page 187*
	Familiarity breeds contempt – films that have lost the plot *Page 189*
	Why are soaps so popular? *Page 190*
	Football is a great way to defeat the racists - The Mirror *Page 193*
	Jay-Z: The Hustler - The Independent *Page 195*
Reviews	Console: Playstation 3 or Wii? www.helium.com *Page 198*
	Films: Quiz Show/Wagons East/Coraline/Hannah Montana *Page 200*
	Books: Bootleg/Going Straight/The Summerhouse *Page 205*

Chapter 1 — Introduction

How can I improve through using this book?
This book aims to develop your skills as a sophisticated writer who is able to organise your thoughts in a clear and imaginative way in order to impact on your audience and achieve your purpose. Each chapter will consist of a range of challenges which should support your journey to become a more effective writer.

How is it organised?
Each chapter will consist of a range of challenges which will develop your

- *thinking skills;*
- *understanding of how to write effectively for a range of purposes and audiences;*
- *understanding of how to succeed (what good looks like);*
- *future skills – how you can apply the skills developed outside of school.*

There is also a section in each chapter (Personalised Progression) in which you will be able to reflect on what level you are working and get advice on how to move to the next level.

An effective writer is someone who
- has a clear purpose in mind;
- therefore chooses the correct words;
- at the right time;
- with the appropriate layout and language features;
- in the appropriate context;
- which impacts on the target audience;
- therefore achieving the intended purpose.

Chapter 1

Responding to a writing question.

It is important to develop skills in reading the question carefully and plan your answer effectively.

The question below has been annotated to reveal how you can quickly establish a connection with the task.

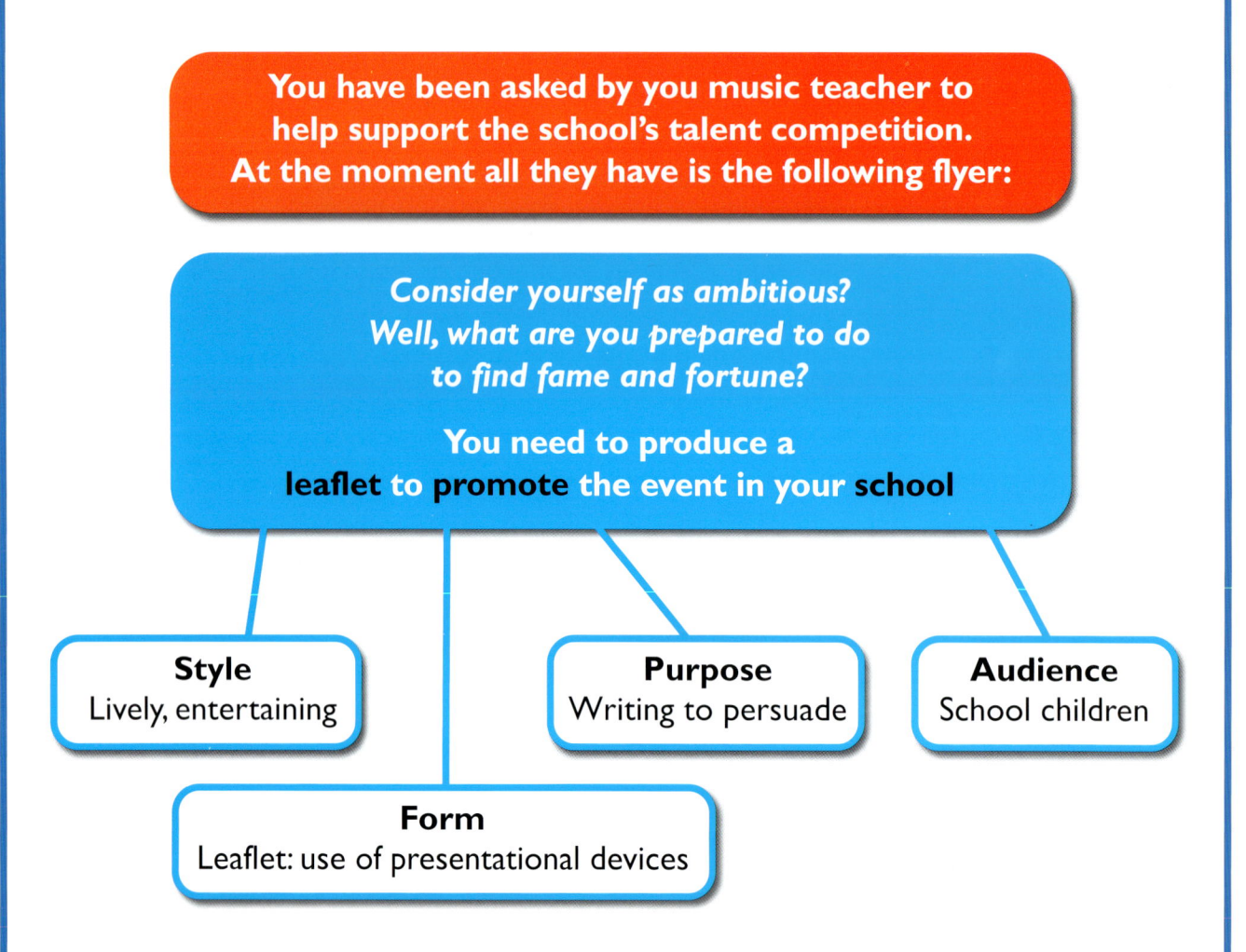

> You have been asked by you music teacher to help support the school's talent competition. At the moment all they have is the following flyer:

> *Consider yourself as ambitious? Well, what are you prepared to do to find fame and fortune?*
>
> *You need to produce a **leaflet** to promote the event in your school*

Style
Lively, entertaining

Purpose
Writing to persuade

Audience
School children

Form
Leaflet: use of presentational devices

Connecting your ideas

On the next few pages are a range of connectives that you can use when writing effectively. These will be explored at length throughout this text book.

It is vitally important that when you make vocabulary choices, that your decision is based on the context/purpose/audience; this is so your writing can have the maximum impact. (Don't choose an ambitious 'big word' unless you understand its meaning).

Chapter 1

Connective Bank

Sequence	Cause and Effect	Contrast and balance	Opinion and interpretation
Initially to begin with	consequently	but	it would seem
first(ly)	thus	however	one might consider/suggest
then	so	nevertheless	propose/deduce/infer
so far	hence	alternatively	presumably
after(wards)	as a result	to turn to	in the view of
at last (lastly)	because/as	yet	on the strength of
finally	therefore	despite this	to the best of one's belief
once	accordingly	on the contrary	theoretically
secondly (etc)	since/until	as for	literally
next	whenever	the opposite	obviously
subsequently	as long as	still	possibly
meanwhile	effectively	instead	maybe
at length	of course	on the other hand	contrary to
in the end	depending upon	whereas	improbably
eventually	necessarily	otherwise	incredibly
succeeding	eventually	although	
following	inevitably	apart from	
since/prior to	it may happen that	equally	
previously later	in the course of things	to balance this	
		all the same	
		for all that	
		albeit/though	
		taking one thing with another	
		it is doubtful	
		disputing this	

Chapter 1 — Connective Bank

Addition	Illustration	Comparison	Persuasion
and	for example	equally	of course
also	for instance	similarly	naturally
further (more)	such as	compared with	obviously
too	as	comparatively	clearly
again	as revealed by	an equivalent	evidently
the following	thus	in the same way	surely
and then	to show that	likewise	certainly
what is more	to take the case of	as with	decidedly
moreover	to elucidate	to balance this	indeed
as well as	that is to say	in juxtaposition	virtually
to complement	in other words	by way of contrast	no wonder
	a case in point	in contrast	strangely enough
	an instance		oddly enough
			luckily
			(un)fortunately
			admittedly
			undoubtedly

Restriction	Emphasis	Summary	Conclusion
only if	above all	in brief	to conclude
unless	in particular	in short	in conclusion
except (for)	notably	on the whole	after all
save (for)	specifically	in all	finally
	especially	overall	when all is said and done
	significantly	to sum up	in the end
	more importantly	in summary	ultimately
	indeed / explicitly	to recapitulate	
	in fact	in a nutshell	
		in conclusion	

Chapter 1

It is vitally important that you remember that:

- allowing time for thinking and discussion greatly improves your writing;
- reading widely informs your writing;
- experimenting with vocabulary is an excellent way of practising your skills;
- producing effective writing should have a real audience and purpose in mind;
- finding your own voice and style will give your work originality and flair;
- planning, redrafting and refining are essential ingredients of being an accomplished writer.

Chapter 2 — Creative Licence

Programme of Study Links	**Creativity** - Making fresh connections between ideas, experiences, texts and words.
Framework Objectives	**7.1** - generating ideas, planning and drafting **7.2** - using and adapting the conventions and forms of texts on paper and on screen **8.1a** - develop character and voice in fiction writing
Thinking Skills	**Creative thinking skills** **Enquiry**
AFL	Sharing of learning objectives and success criteria
Assessment Focus	**AF1** - write imaginative, interesting and thoughtful texts **AF7** - select appropriate and effective vocabulary
Assessment Focus	Producing writing for contexts and purposes beyond the classroom

Challenge 1 - Get thinking

In threes, allocate the following roles:

a) explainer (someone who gives a definition of the following words)
b) challenger (someone who ask questions of the explainer as to why they have made their decisions)
c) recorder (someone who records/writes down a summary of each response)

1) A&B need to discuss the following words and consider the first thoughts that enter their heads when reading them out. C records the thoughts.

- Script
- Story
- Poetry
- Song

2) What came from this discussion? What would you consider as the main similarities and differences between these types of writing? How important do you think talk for writing is?

What has helped me learn effectively today?

Chapter 2

In this unit I will learn how to effectively… *(Learning Objectives)*	• generate ideas and plan effectively in a range of forms • develop a character and voice in fiction writing
The topics I will be studying are… *(Stimulus)*	• Prose writing • Poetry • Scriptwriting
My understand will be checked by seeing how I… *(Assessment Criteria)*	AF1 – write imaginative, interesting and thoughtful texts AF7 – select appropriate and effective vocabulary
My achievement will be demonstrated through me successfully completing the following challenges: *(Learning Outcomes)*	1. Get thinking (image) 2. Response to blank page 3. Planning for writing 4. Applying planning skills 5. Plot analysis 6. Film task 7. Original character 8. Image sketch 9. Image activity 10. Improve sentence 11. Descriptive task 12. Fill in middle part of story 13. Toolbox matching exercise 14. Eveline dramatic reading 15. Eveline role play 16. Eveline's journey 17. Effective description 18. Character voice through poetry 19. Stephen Lawrence response 20. Poetry development activity 21. Euthanasia poetry response 22. Sonnet writing 23. Radio script 24. TV script Future Skills – adapting prose to script

Chapter 2

Challenge 2

What strategies could I use to progress further?

Generating ideas for writing

With a partner, discuss how it would feel if you received the following piece of paper:

Produce a piece of creative writing below

_____
_____
_____
_____
_____
_____

What's the problem?

Well, perhaps it is the blank page syndrome, a condition that affects many students when asked to produce a piece of creative writing without any stimulus or opportunity to generate ideas or plan effectively

How can I generate ideas?

There is not one, definitive way of generating ideas for writing although often the task itself will give hints as to where to get information from (particularly non-fiction writing) As well as researching a topic and ensuring that you write in the correct style you also need some strategies which will help you generate ideas, particularly for open-ended creative writing when there is not an obvious theme or subject matter.

Using the media – newspapers/adverts/internet etc is an obvious method though it is more important that you **find your own voice** through your writing. Good writers are those who **impose their own style** and bring their **own personality and background** to a writing task, rather than trying to replicate someone else's ideas.

In non-fiction, planning should involve generating a range of facts and opinions (including your own) on a given topic and adapting your language and style to suit the needs of your target audience.

In fiction writing, some people are able to carefully plan in terms of how each scene/stanza/paragraph is laid out; each character/setting described etc. However, others work best from simply starting in a powerful way which then creates the stimulus and structure for everything else to fall in place. As will be explored later on in this chapter, effective stories should consider the characters' goals and obstacles, as well as the consequences of their actions which will often lead to a complication and crises.

Chapter 2 — Challenge 3

Planning for writing

Here is a table which takes you through the process that is involved in effectively planning for writing. As you look through each section, rate each one in terms of how often you consider this. 1 **always**, 2 **sometimes**, 3 **never**.

Planning for Writing

Persona	**Who are you?** Have you been asked to write from your own personal viewpoint (i.e. a KS3 student) or have you been asked to adopt the viewpoint of someone else? (i.e a character from a novel / a policeman writing a report). These questions often begin with 'Imagine you are' or 'You have been asked to be a…'
Purpose	**Why are you writing this?** Is it to… Inform Argue Explain Persuade Describe Advise Explore Analyse Imagine Review Entertain Comment
Audience	**Who is it for?** Age groups Gender Interest groups (smokers/pensioners/car owners)
Content **Use of facts and opinions**	**Facts** **Opinions** Will any statistics support your points? Will giving your own view help your writing task? Will any true stories help to achieve your purpose and appeal to your audience? Do you have any anecdotes (personal stories) which may help to support your point of view?
Style and tone	**Should it be…** serious/ light-hearted /entertaining/ assertive/ persuasive/ sensitive/objective/subjective/ironic/satirical?
Layout	**Do you need to use any of the following?** Varied font size Photographs Logos Bullet points Pictures Slogans Headings/subheadings Captions Graphics

In what other subjects could I apply these skills?

Chapter 2

Sequence	Should your writing be in a particular order? Chronological/flash back
Viewpoint	Does your writing need to be in the *1st person* I wish I could do more to help the homeless *2nd person* You can do more to help the homeless *3rd person* She wanted to do more to help the homeless (or a combination of these?)
Tense	Which tense is most appropriate? Past, Present or both
Voice	Passive – The election was won by a landslide by Obama Active – Obama won the election by a landslide
Sentence type	Which of the following sentence types are most appropriate? *(You may well need a combination of these types)* **Statements** The homeless suffer on the streets **Commands** You must help the homeless **Questions** (as well as rhetorical questions) Can you sit there and let them suffer? **Exclamation** It's a disgrace that they have to suffer while we live in our cosy houses!
Sentence structure and length	Do you need to focus on using one or more of these types of sentences? **Simple** a sentence with only one clause (or main ideas) *Burny shot wide of the target* **Compound** a sentence which has two or more main clauses of equal length *Burny shot wide of the target but Mugsy saved the day by scoring the winner.* **Complex** a sentence which has at least one main clause and one or more subordinate clause (a clause that is dependent on the main clause) *Burny shot wide of the target because he was too busy moaning at others.*
Key words and phrases to use	What type of vocabulary is required? descriptive/factual/ subject specific/ rhetorical

Chapter 2 — Challenge 4

Applying your planning skills

a) Read through the following questions and for each one, devise a writing frame which you think would most effectively complete the task.
b) Using your own writing frame or the Planning for Writing grid on the previous pages, produce a detailed plan for one of these questions.
c) Swap your plan with a learning partner and ask them to complete the writing task.
d) Once completed, provide feedback on how helpful (or otherwise) the plans were. Make suggestions on how it could have been improved.

1	Talented, enthusiastic and hard working student needed for lead role in Revenge is Sweet. Your character seeks power and revenge at all costs, no matter who gets in their way. Please send application letter addressed to the Head of Drama.
2	Are you ambitious? Do you want to get to the top of your chosen career? What does it take to get to the top/ Does it matter who you upset or have to stand on to get your own way? Write a speech to your careers adviser in which you comment on the theme of ambition. You want to make the point that being successful does not mean you need to 'stamp' on people along the way.
3	War is pointless, mindless yet sometimes necessary. Argue for and against the reasons why Britain goes to war.
4	Describe a time in which you were let down by somebody yet came back to succeed against all the odds.
5	Write a lively and entertaining review about a horror film/TV programme for your school magazine.

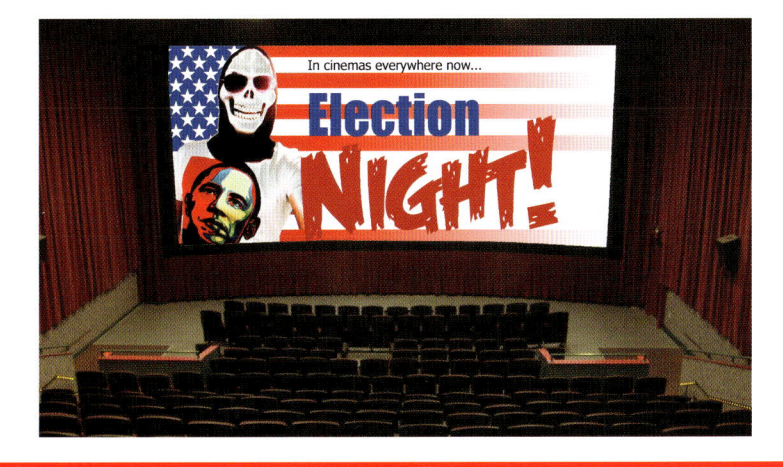

When could I use these skills outside of school?

Chapter 2 — Challenge 5

Developing viewpoint, voice and ideas

Storytelling – the basic plots

Even though there are probably millions of different stories that have been told all around the world, there are essentially seven main plots which all stories relate to in some way.

As you read through these think of a book/poem/film that you have recently read/watched and consider how these plots apply to the plot.

1) **Overcoming the monster**
   A community is under threat and a hero overcomes a series of barriers to save the people, often winning the treasure or the heart of a loved one.

   An example of this would be **The Lion King** in that Simba eventually avenges his father's death (Mufasa) by defeating the monstrous threat (his Uncle Scar) and rescues his community (the Pride lands) whilst winning the heart of Nala.

2) **Rags to riches**
   A young hero or heroine overcomes enormous difficulties in their environment (living conditions) and those around them (could be a jealous family member) A series of adventures leads to a crisis, though due to the character's new found strength, they overcome this and are rewarded for their honest efforts.

   An example of this would be **Cinderella** who is treated poorly by her jealous step sisters yet eventually is rewarded through her perseverance and fulfils her dream (marrying the Prince)

3) **The quest**
   A hero or heroine needs to find something precious which could be treasure or a safe passage home. Their journey and mission is long and hazardous which involves many set backs along the way though eventually the hero achieves their objective.

   An example of this would be in **Lord of the Rings.**

4) **Voyage and return**
   A hero or heroine is taken out of their familiar surroundings into a world which is alien to them (it could be past/present or simply fantastical) Initially, this could be an exhilarating experience though dangers creep up on them which leads the character to seek an escape to their own world and comfort zone.
   Examples include **Alice in Wonderland** and **Where the Wild Things are.**

5) **Comedy**
   A character (or a series of characters) have barriers put in their way due to confusion or misunderstanding. There is the potential for tragedy though eventually the confusion becomes entangled and the situation is transformed and the characters are brought together for a happy union (often a romantic one)

Examples of this can be seen in most Hollywood romantic comedies, particularly those including weddings.

What has helped me learn effectively today?

Chapter 2

6) **Tragedy**
The main character (protagonist) is unfulfilled and seeks greater power which they initially achieve; however, through their greed in wanting further gratification, forces begin to get in their way then their world begins to fall around them, leading to their eventual and inevitable demise.

7) **Rebirth**
A young hero or heroine falls under the influence of a dark power and becomes imprisoned by this power for a long time; seemingly, the dark power has triumphed though eventually they are released from these dark forces and are saved by a hero or change of fortune.

Examples of this include *Snow White*, *A Christmas Carol*.
It is important that in whatever story you produce the key thing to explore is how your characters attempt to **overcome barriers** in order to achieve their **objective**. The **complications** that arise along the way creates the **tension** and leads to the **climax** and the eventual **resolution**.

Challenge 6

In pairs, choose a film that you are both very familiar with and copy out and complete the table below:

Film name:	
Hero/heroine/main character(s) are…	
Their objective is to…	
The obstacles in their way are:	
They try and overcome their obstacles through…	
The complications they find along their journey are…	
This leads to the climax of…	
It is resolved by…	

What strategies could I use to progress further?

Chapter 2

How to create realistic and memorable characters

As mentioned earlier, the success of writing effective stories lies in the reader being able to identify with the main character(s) in your story; this does not mean we have to like them, though they need to have an appeal to them which helps capture your reader's attention.

In terms of description, below are some examples of the kind of elements you could include:

Descriptions of their

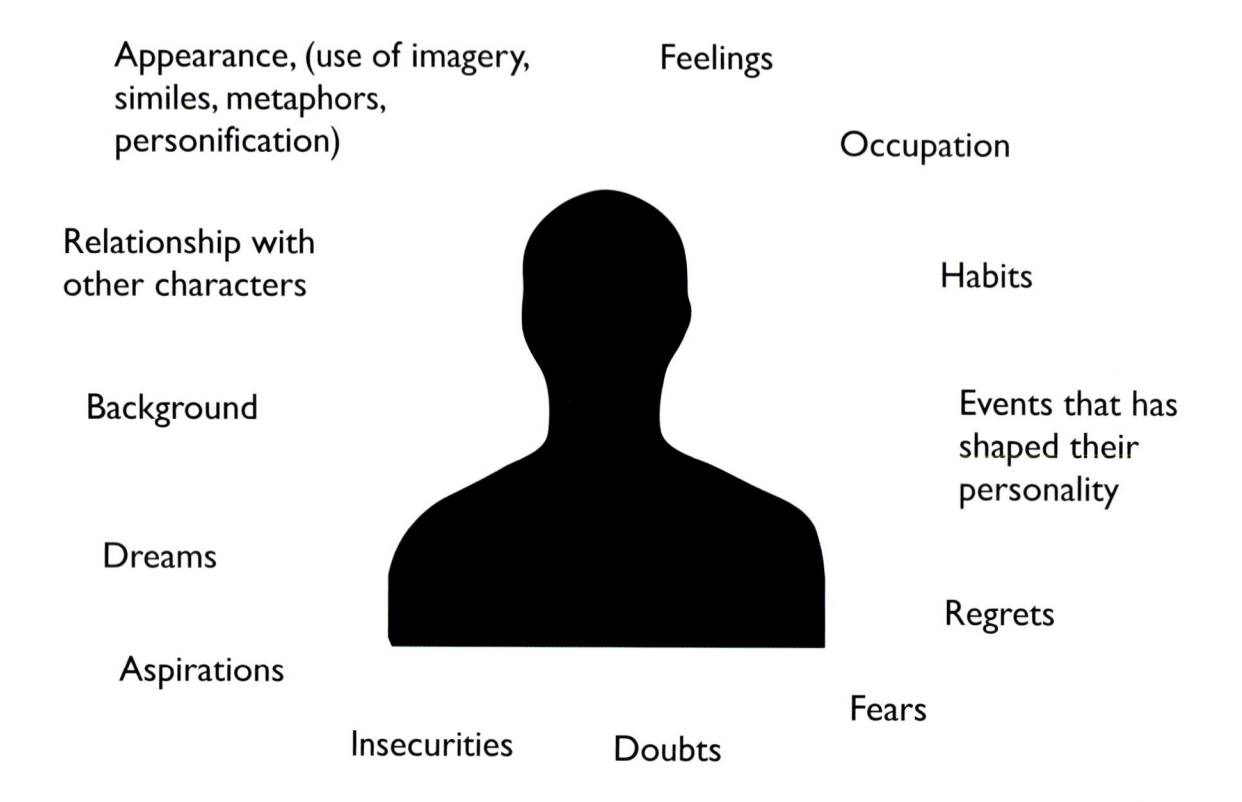

- Appearance, (use of imagery, similes, metaphors, personification)
- Feelings
- Occupation
- Relationship with other characters
- Habits
- Background
- Events that has shaped their personality
- Dreams
- Regrets
- Aspirations
- Fears
- Insecurities
- Doubts

We also learn about characters through

- the way they speak (tone of voice/use of formal language/ slang);
- how they react to events around them;
- how they compare with other characters;
- their role in the story. (victim/villain/hero?);
- what other characters say about them;
- what the author (you) says about them.

Chapter 2 — Challenge 7

Create an original character using the techniques in the table below:

Characteristics	Description of your imaginative character
Appearance,	
Feelings	
Relationship with other characters	
Background	
Events that has shaped their personality	
Occupation	
Habits	
Aspirations	
Insecurities	
Doubts	
Fears	
Regrets	
The way they speak	
How they react to events around them	
How they compare with other characters	
Their role in the story.	
What other characters say about them	
What the author (you) says about them.	

In what other subjects could I apply these skills?

Chapter 2

Challenge 8

Using imagery effectively

As you read through the passage, draw a rough sketch on each image that the writer uses.

> James walked slowly, thoughtfully, almost trance like through the prison gates-St. Mark's Roman Catholic School etched treacherously along the arched dome, piercing his saucer eyes. Suddenly, fear surrounded him, holding him ransom, like a hostage approaching his first day captive. As he shuffled towards the chains, a blurred image of hope waved at him, through the murky future ahead. "Your James aren't you?" It was Michelle, the girl he thought he'd lost to St Elizabeth's and here she was loosening the chains, and releasing him from his lonely lighthouse.

Challenge 9

Think of a series of images that would describe a new experience that you have recently encountered and produce a sentence on each image which helps to describe your feelings during this time.

Challenge 10

Improve the following sentence, using the techniques demonstrated above.
Martin was a boy who went on holiday, met up with his friends, had a terrible time and came home later than expected.

Vocabulary choices should be ambitious

Your word choice should extend the descriptions of settings, characters and mood. Avoid over using typical phrases such as…
Cold as ice/ Green as grass/ It was a cold, dark night.

Be original in your ideas

Descriptions could be of one or more of the following, depending on the task set.
- Surroundings – using the senses in a literal way and metaphorical way.

For example:

Literal	Metaphorical
I could taste the searing sweat gently brooding over my crippled gums	*As I entered all I could taste was fear, running between my gums.*

- Your thoughts and feelings
  Loneliness crept up beside me.
- Your past and how its affected your current situation.
  Perhaps the attention I always craved was now being satisfied.
- Your hopes and fears.
  Maybe now, with all that's gone before, I could be forgiven, if not forgotten.

When could I use these skills outside of school?

What has helped me learn effectively today?

Chapter 2

In the following extract, Tom has been asked to describe what he did at the weekend in an entertaining way. He decided to use similes, metaphors and personification to help the reader identify with how he must have been feeling at different points during the weekend.

Key moments	Similes	Metaphors	Personification
Leaving School (Friday)	I felt like a lottery winner waiting for its prize.	I was a balloon that was filling up.	Joy was bouncing in front of me waiting to be caught.
Going to town	I felt like a tiger waiting to get my claws round some meat.	I was a thermometer getting hotter and hotter ready to explode as I ran to the shop.	The video was dancing before me getting further and further away.
Going to Southport (Sunday)	As I stepped on to the beach I felt like a dog with a bone.	I was a Chameleon hiding in the leaves.	Freedom pulsated me to the open air.
Going to see Kyle Minogue (Sunday)	I was as happy as a bird propelling through the open air.		Anticipation slid between my toes.
Going to bed (Sunday night)	I was as content as a kitten's first sight of its loving mother.		A gentle feeling of sadness engulfed me as the haunting gates blurred back into my vision.

Can you think of an effective metaphor to describe how Tom might have been feeling at the concert and going to bed?

Chapter 2 — Challenge 11

Using the same techniques as Tom, think about how you could effectively describe your weekend – notice how even the most basic of events (going to sleep) has been described effectively to create a particular feeling.

Enticing your reader

Your main purpose as a creative writer is to engage your reader which often means leaving as much out, as in; in other words, you as the writer should be in full possession of how the characters will develop and how the plot will unfold though it is best to drip out the information at key moments to draw your reader in and excite their imagination.

Read through the opening chapter of the novel *Holes* by Louis Sachar and consider how you as a reader are immediately drawn into the story.

> There is no lake at Camp Green Lake. There once was a very large lake here, the largest lake in Texas. That was over a hundred years ago. Now it is just a dry, flat wasteland.
>
> There used to be a town of Green Lake as well. The town shrivelled and dried up along with the lake, and the people who lived there.
> During the summer the daytime temperature hovers around ninety-five degrees in the shade-if you can find any shade. There's not much shade in a big dry lake.
>
> The only trees are two old oaks on the eastern edge of the "lake." A hammock is stretched between the two trees, and a log cabin stands behind that.
>
> The campers are forbidden to lie in the hammock. It belongs to the Warden. The Warden owns the shade. Out on the lake, rattlesnakes and scorpions find shade under rocks and in the holes dug by the campers. Here's a good rule to remember about rattlesnakes and scorpions: If you don't bother them, they won't bother you. Usually.
>
> Being bitten by a scorpion or even a rattlesnake is not the worst thing that can happen to you. You won't die. Usually. Sometimes a camper will try to be bitten by a scorpion, or even a small rattlesnake. Then he will get to spend a day or two recovering in his tent, instead of having to dig a hole out on the lake. But you don't want to be bitten by a yellow-spotted lizard. That's the worst thing that can happen to you. You will die a slow and painful death. Always.
> If you get bitten by a yellow spotted lizard, you might as well go into the shade of the oak trees and lie in the hammock. There is nothing anyone can do to you anymore.

What strategies could I use to progress further?

Chapter 2

Enticing your reader

Read through the notes made below which considers how Louis Sachar subtly engages the reader.

There is no lake at Camp Green Lake. There once was a very large lake here, the largest lake in Texas. That was over a hundred years ago. Now it is just a dry, flat wasteland. There used to be a town of Green Lake as well. The town shrivelled and dried up along with the lake, and the people who lived there.

During the summer the daytime temperature hovers around ninety-five degrees in the shade-if you can find any shade. There's not much shade in a big dry lake. The only trees are two old oakes on the eastern edge of the "lake." A hammock is stretched between the two trees, and a log cabin stands behind that.

The campers are forbidden to lie in the hammock. It belongs to the Warden. The Warden owns the shade. Out on the lake, rattlesnakes and scorpions find shade under rocks and in the holes dug by the campers. Here's a good rule to remember about rattlesnakes and scorpions: If you don't bother them, they won't bother you. Usually.

Being bitten by a scorpion or even a rattlesnake is not the worst thing that can happen to you. You won't die. Usually. Sometimes a camper will try to be bitten by a scorpion, or even a small rattlesnake. Then he will get to spend a day or two recovering in his tent, instead of having to dig a hole out on the lake. But you don't want to be bitten by a yellow-spotted lizard. That's the worst thing that can happen to you. You will die a slow and painful death. Always.
If you get bitten by a yellow spotted lizard, you might as well go into the shade of the oak trees and lie in the hammock. There is nothing anyone can do to you anymore.

No lake/no town – gets the reader thinking of why/how come/how could that have happened?

shrivelled - effective verb to create the decaying image.

The campers are forbidden to lie in the hammock Now some characters are introduced – described as campers – is it a holiday camp?

It belongs to the Warden. The Warden owns the shade. Now we realise that is must be some kind of prison camp.

One word sentence creates the sombre atmosphere as well as the rather flat narrative style.

Chapter 2

Using description effectively

Your description should be vivid, realistic and thought provoking. The reader should want to ask questions as they read not find out all the answers. All description must allow the reader to visualise the environment the character's are in as well as being able to identify with the characters' predicament. Soaps on TV work because we usually love or hate the characters.

For this challenge, you need to use your imagination to visualise how the events may have taken place. The opening and ending have been completed for you.

Follow the plan on the next page to support your writing

Beginning
Something woke her from a deep but disturbed sleep. She was never quite sure what that something had been – a cold gust from an open window, a memory rekindled by the smell of burnt cloth that now hung in the air – but she would spend her whole life wishing that she could only have stayed sleeping for another hour or so. With the air of paid cleaner going about her routine daily business, she rose stiffly from her small wicker chair and began to deal with the blood-spattered broken glass that covered the pale gold carpet…

End
The weight of shame would be there forever, pulling at his legs with every weary step, like a sad old dog overdue for its morning walk. At the same time his mind felt clean and full of direction, as it had never done before. I wish you'd never learned to weep – pure and simple every time…The song swept along on the muffled café jukebox, as sweet tears splashed onto the filthy beige floor.

Mark Boardman

Chapter 2 — Challenge 12

Fill in the middle parts of this narrative in order to link the beginning and ending

Planning your response

Before you begin writing the middle part you must ask yourself why the two characters feel the way that they do and why are they described in such a way? Answer the following questions and try to be as imaginative and realistic as possible.

Beginning

- What has woken her from her sleep?
- Why was it deep and disturbed?
- What could the memory have been?
- Why could she smell burnt cloth in the air?
- Why does she wish she could have stayed asleep for an hour longer?
- Why does she go about her daily business like a paid cleaner?
- Why does she rise stiffly from the chair?
- Why is there blood splattered broken glass around her?

Ending

- Why does he feel the weight of shame upon himself?
- Why does his mind still feel clean and full of direction despite his shame?
- Why had his mind never felt so clear before?
- Why does that particular song have a big affect on him?
- Why is he crying? Why are his tears described as being sweet?

Let's remind ourselves of the tools used by writers.

- sentence structure – short/long/beginning with the emotions or dramatic verbs/ effective use of punctuation etc.
- varied vocabulary
- use of persuasive/emotive/dynamic language
- use of senses
- use of imagery
- comparisons
- repetition
- contrast
- personification
- hooking devices

In what other subjects could I apply these skills?

Chapter 2 — Challenge 13

Read through the following sentences and in pairs complete the following tasks.
1) Discuss which tools are being used (there are often more than one).
2) How could the sentences be improved?

a) Insecurity held her ransom
b) The taste of sweat slowly trickled down his brooding, now grief ridden lips.
c) Home seemed such a beautiful comfort to her, especially as she now considered the glowing fire, the welcoming hug of granddad and the luxurious carpeted lounge, just longing for her arrival.
d) Her eyes were a blue ocean of sparkling blue diamonds, shimmering in the summer breeze.
e) Benarbia Boost for Bewildered Blues.
f) He was as isolated as a lighthouse without the beam of hope.
g) Who was it? Stop thinking about it, the footsteps, the footsteps getting louder, louder by the minute. Who is it? Who's there?
h) The air was sweet with sunshine, homing in on my eager limbs.
i) Facially, she was a strange combination of a witch's frown and a cry for help.
j) But wait – this was it. I have finally made it. Is this the end?
k) His guilt seemed to be invading him, yet his inner strength pushed it to one side once more.
l) The forest was thick with the darkest mist you could imagine; black, sickly fog which reflected the inhabitants.

When could I use these skills outside of school?

Chapter 2

Creating powerful character

In the following passage are extracts from a short story by James Joyce titled *Eveline* which explores the dilemma that a young girl faces when offered the chance to leave Dublin and begin a new life in Buenos Aires (in Argentina) Joyce is able to powerfully draw the reader into the world of Eveline through his description of the environment that she lives in as well as revealing her troubled state of mind as she attempts to make the decision.

Challenge 14

In a small group, read through this passage, and take on the roles of looking closely at how Joyce describes Eveline's

- physical environment;
- past;
- relationship with her father;
- hopes & fears;
- final decision and feelings at the end.

Eveline

Home! She looked round the room, reviewing all its familiar objects which she had dusted once a week for so many years, wondering where on earth all the dust came from. Perhaps she would never see again those familiar objects from which she had never dreamed of being divided. And yet during all those years she had never found out the name of the priest whose yellowing photograph hung on the wall above the broken harmonium beside the coloured print of the promises made to Blessed Margaret Mary Alacoque. He had been a school friend of her father. Whenever he showed the photograph to a visitor her father used to pass it with a casual word:

'He is in Melbourne now.'

She had consented to go away, to leave her home. Was that wise? She tried to weigh each side of the question. In her home anyway she had shelter and food; she had those whom she had known all her life about her. Of course she had to work hard, both in the house and at business. What would they say of her in the Stores when they found out that she had run away with a fellow? Say she was a fool, perhaps; and her place would be filled up by advertisement. Miss Gavan would be glad. She had always had an edge on her, especially whenever there were people listening.

'Miss Hill, don't you see these ladies are waiting?'
'Look lively, Miss Hill, please.'

Chapter 2

She would not cry many tears at leaving the Stores.
But in her new home, in a distant unknown country, it would not be like that. Then she would be married - she, Eveline. People would treat her with respect then. She would not be treated as her mother had been. Even now, though she was over nineteen, she sometimes felt herself in danger of her father's violence. She knew it was that that had given her the Palpitations. When they were growing up he had never gone for her, like he used to go for Harry and Ernest, because she was a girl; but latterly he had begun to threaten her and say what he would do to her only for her dead mother's sake. And now she had nobody to protect her, Ernest was dead and Harry, who was in the church decorating business, was nearly always down somewhere in the country.

She had hard work to keep the house together and to see that the two young children who had been left to her charge went to school regularly and got their meals regularly. It was hard work - a hard life - but now that she was about to leave it she did not find it a wholly undesirable life.

She was about to explore another life with Frank. Frank was very kind, manly, open-hearted. She was to go away with him by the night-boat to be his wife and to live with him in Buenos Aires, where he had a home waiting for her. He had fallen on his feet in Buenos Aires, he said, and had come over to the old country just for a holiday. Of course, her father had found out the affair and had forbidden her to have anything to say to him. 'I know these sailor chaps,' he said. One day he had quarrelled with Frank, and after that she had to meet her lover secretly.

She stood up in a sudden impulse of terror. Escape! She must escape! Frank would save her. He would give her life, perhaps love, too. But she wanted to live. Why should she be unhappy? She had a right to happiness. Frank would take her in his arms, fold her in his arms. He would save her.

She stood among the swaying crowd in the station at the North Wall. He held her hand and she knew that he was speaking to her, saying something about the passage over and over again. The station was full of soldiers with brown baggages. Through the wide doors of the sheds she caught a glimpse of the black mass of the boat, lying in beside the quay wall, with illumined portholes.

She felt her cheek pale and cold and, out of a maze of distress, she prayed to God to direct her, to show her what was her duty. The boat blew a long mournful whistle into the mist. If she went, tomorrow she would be on the sea with Frank, steaming towards Buenos Aires. Their passage had been booked. Could she still draw back after all he had done for her? Her distress awoke a nausea in her body and she kept moving her lips in silent fervent prayer.

Chapter 2

A bell clanged upon her heart. She felt him seize her hand: 'Come!'
All the seas of the world tumbled about her heart. He was drawing her into them: he would drown her. She gripped with both hands at the iron railing.
'Come!'

No! No! No! It was impossible. Her hands clutched the iron in frenzy. Amid the seas she sent a cry of anguish.
'Eveline! Evvy!'

He rushed beyond the barrier and called to her to follow. He was shouted at to go on, but he still called to her. She set her white face to him, passive, like a helpless animal. Her eyes gave him no sign of love or farewell or recognition.

How did Joyce manage to create Eveline's world so effectively?

One of the main skills needed to be an effective writer is to create a world so convincingly that the reader enters it, involves themselves in it, and ultimately is gripped with the characters' dilemmas.
This is true of Eveline in that Joyce creates the complex world of Eveline very precisely so that we can fully appreciate how difficult her decision is to leave Dublin and seek a new life elsewhere.

Challenge 15

In threes, take on the following roles and provide the reasons why Eveline should stay or leave. You need to consider the arguments from your point of view as that character.

- Eveline
- Eveline's father
- Frank

Joyce uses imagery effectively to create Eveline's world; this also adds to the decaying and depressing atmosphere which makes the reader empathise with Eveline's plight and therefore makes us desperate for her to escape. When she finally decides she is unable to leave and will therefore be trapped forever, we can almost feel her pain and despair.
A powerful way of creating atmosphere is through using imagery when describing the environment, particuallry when you make it multi layered as in the example on the next page:

What strategies could I use to progress further?

Chapter 2

| And yet during all those years she had never found out the name of the priest whose ==yellowing== photograph hung on the wall above the ==broken== harmonium beside the coloured print of the ==promises== made to Blessed Margaret Mary Alacoque | There are references here made to the disappointments that she has faced. The choice of adjectives 'yellowing' and 'broken' help to create the sense of despair. Joyce has described these objects next to the 'promises made' to Blessed Mary Alocoque to suggest that promises are never kept in Eveline's world. |

Identifying with a character's journey

As mentioned earlier, it is vital that you engage your reader so that they want to go on the journey of your main character(s). Joyce takes us through these conflicts and contradictions that Eveline is facing which makes her final decision to stay all the more dramatic.

Challenge 16

In a small group, you need to plot Eveline's 'journey' from her starting point to her final decision. You could view Eveline's journey as being on a ring road or roundabout, in other words, going nowhere eventually.

1) Copy out the table below and consider how Eveline decides to stay.

Starting journey	Reasons persuading her to		Final destination
Home	Stay	Leave	Home

How could I use this technique in my own writing?

It is important that if you want your reader to feel involved in your story and care about what happens to your characters, you need to create the world around them.

Look through the table below and try out using this technique when creating characters in your story.

The world of Eveline	
Her environment (and how it is described)	Role in society
Past	Treatment by others
Relationship with father	Decisions made
Role in the family	Hopes & fears

In what other subjects could I apply these skills?

Chapter 2

Using contrast effectively to create character

In the following extract from *Hard Times*, Charles Dickens effectively uses contrast to reveal the characters of Sissy Jupe and Bitzer through the strict, uncompromising teacher, Mr. Gradgrind.

Firstly, how do the names of the characters suggest their individual personalities?

Try using names that reflect your characters' personality.

Mr. Gradgrind, Bitzer, Sissy Jupe

The square finger, moving here and there, lighted suddenly on Bitzer, perhaps because he chanced to sit in the same ray of sunlight which, darting in at one of the bare windows of the intensely white-washed room, irradiated Sissy. For, the boys and girls sat on the face of the inclined plane in two compact bodies, divided up the centre by a narrow interval; and Sissy, being at the corner of a row on the sunny side, came in for the beginning of a sunbeam, of which Bitzer, being at the corner of a row on the other side, a few rows in advance, caught the end.	The square finger, moving here and there, suggests intimidation white-washed room hints at cold atmosphere
But, whereas the girl was so dark-eyed and dark-haired, that she seemed to receive a deeper and more lustrous colour from the sun, when it shone upon her, the boy was so light-eyed and light-haired that the self-same rays appeared to draw out of him what little colour he ever possessed.	Use of sun as a symbol of how the characters differ greatly Sissy Jupe, full of life and colour. Bitzer, drained of colour and life.
His cold eyes would hardly have been eyes, but for the short ends of lashes which, by bringing them into immediate contrast with something paler than themselves, expressed their form. His short-cropped hair might have been a mere continuation of the sandy freckles on his forehead and face. His skin was so unwholesomely deficient in the natural tinge, that he looked as though, if he were cut, he would bleed white.	Detailed description of Bitzer's pale, unhealthy, unnatural appearance creates him as a victim and someone we would pity.

29

Chapter 2

How could I use this techniques in my own writing? Apply these skills.

When wanting to contrast characters, try using a symbol (such as the sun light coming in) and comment on how the characters react differently to it.

Challenge 17

You own writing

Having looked through how writing can be effective, you now need to have a go at writing your own effective piece of description, using the techniques in the previous few pages.

Remember to use the tools you have – avoid too much dialogue and narration.

1. Describe a place that is both exciting yet frightening.
2. You are trapped physically somehow yet see a small light, describe your movements.
3. Describe a place that is emotionally challenging as it brings up things from your past that you would rather leave behind.
4. Imagine you saw the aftermath of a murder scene. Describe the scene, events and your own feelings.
5. Describe your ideal holiday location, ensuring that you make the place come alive for the reader.

Before you begin, remember to decide on which tools you will use and how you are going to use them.

Developing your voice through poetry

Why would I want to use poetry to communicate my thoughts?

The beauty of using poetry is that it can help shape and organise your thoughts in a way that can often be very creative and powerful. It also allows you to focus more explicitly on the meaning of what you want to communicate, without the need of extending your sentences in great length.

Does it have to rhyme?

No is the short answer, though if using rhyme helps to draw attention to particular words or adds energy or humour to your writing then rhyme is an effective vehicle for this.

How long should a poem be?

This depends on what message you want to get across to your reader. Often shorter poems are more succinct (straight to the point) though longer poems allow for a narrative (story) to develop; it also allows the reader to develop a relationship with the characters in your poem the persona(s).

When could I use these skills outside of school?

Chapter 2

Can I write in different styles?

There are numerous types of poetic styles and it is important that you find your own voice in a poem (what you want to say) before worrying about the structure.

So how would I begin?

There is not one correct way of planning for, or starting a poem, though what is important is that you choose a subject matter that you have a personal involvement in and that you can bring your own thoughts and feelings to; this does not have to be a serious subject matter and could be your humorous take on a subject which may seem meaningless though actually becomes interesting because of the way you approach it. An effective way to get started is to start playing with words and images that are associated with the subject matter you want to explore. Brainstorm your subject matter, put the words that come up in a jumbled order and see what effects are created. For example:

Subject matter: Parents give us no freedom.

Brainstorm: freedom/responsibility/care/trapped/control/worry/love/rights/
Jumbling the words to make the beginning of a poem:

Freedom doesn't care
Or share
Responsibility

Other techniques could include using the same phrase within each line opener. For example:

I love my parents **though wish** they would let me go
I love my room **though wish** it would be a gateway to the world

If you feel that your poems are too long (in sentence length) then strip away the unnecessary words and start again – sometimes the effects are powerful.

In the poem over the page, Charles Causley effectively creates the environment of Timothy Winters through using humour, language devices and rhyme.
In pairs, read this poem out loud and think about
1) What impression do we get of Timothy Winters?
2) What does the writer say about him that creates this impression?

Chapter 2

Timothy Winters

Timothy Winters comes to school
With eyes as wide as a football-pool,
Ears like bombs and teeth like splinters:
A blitz of a boy is Timothy Winters.

His belly is white, his neck is dark,
And his hair is an exclamation-mark.
His clothes are enough to scare a crow
And through his britches the blue winds blow.

When teacher talks he won't hear a word
And he shoots down dead the arithmetic-bird,
He licks the pattern off his plate
And he's not even heard of the Welfare State.

Timothy Winters has bloody feet
And he lives in a house on Suez Street,
He sleeps in a sack on the kithen floor
And they say there aren't boys like him anymore.

Old Man Winters likes his beer
And his missus ran off with a bombardier,
Grandma sits in the grate with a gin
And Timothy's dosed with an aspirin.

The welfare Worker lies awake
But the law's as tricky as a ten-foot snake,
So Timothy Winters drinks his cup
And slowly goes on growing up.

At Morning Prayers the Master helves
for children less fortunate than ourselves,
And the loudest response in the room is when
Timothy Winters roars "Amen!"

So come one angel, come on ten
Timothy Winters says "Amen
Amen amen amen amen."
Timothy Winters, Lord. Amen

Charles Causley

Chapter 2

How could I use these techniques for my own poetry writing?

Firstly, it is important to examine the techniques that Causley uses.

What message does the poet want to get across?

Causley clearly wants the reader to empathise with the plight of Timothy and he does this by powerful use of:

similes	With eyes as wide as a football-pool, Ears like bombs and teeth like splinters:
metaphors	A blitz of a boy his hair is an exclamation-mark. And he shoots down dead the arithmetic-bird,
adjectives	His belly is white, his neck is dark, Timothy Winters has bloody feet
alliteration	And through his britches the blue winds blow. The welfare Worker lies awake
description of environment	He sleeps in a sack on the kitchen floor He licks the pattern off his plate And Timothy's dosed with an aspirin.
relationship with others	When teacher talks he won't hear a word Old Man Winters likes his beer And his missus ran off with a bombardier, Grandma sits in the grate with a gin
repetition	So come one angel, come on ten Timothy Winters says "Amen Amen amen amen amen." Timothy Winters, Lord. Amen

Chapter 2

Challenge 18 - Applying these skills

Creating your own character's voice through poetry

Try using these techniques when producing a poem about someone you know (or yourself) who goes to school or work (or anywhere); they could be real or imaginary, though remember not to write anything that could offend someone in your school!

For example, you could write:
Jonathan Morgan goes back home; With eyes as static as his garden gnome

Using poetry to present an argument

In the following poems, the poets use their writing as a vehicle to present their views on issues that they feel strongly about.

Benjamin Zephaniah on racism

Stephen Lawrence was a black British teenager from South-East London who was stabbed to death while waiting for a bus on the evening of 22 April 1993. After the initial investigation, five suspects were arrested but never convicted.

In this poem, Benjamin Zephaniah uses his power as a poet to reveal his anger at the way the Stephen Lawrence trial was conducted.

Challenge 19

As you read through this poem, think about what techniques are used by the poet to create such a powerful effect on the reader.

In particular, consider how the following are developed:

- repetition
- similes/metaphors
- powerful verbs
- rhetorical questions

What has helped me learn effectively today?

What strategies could I use to progress further?

Chapter 2

What Stephen Lawrence Has Taught Us

We know who the killers are,
We have watched them strut before us
As proud as sick Mussolinis.
We have watched them strut before us
Compassionless and arrogant,
They paraded before us,
Like angels of death
Protected by the law.

It is now an open secret
Black people do not have
Chips on their shoulders,
They just have injustice on their backs
And justice on their minds,
And now we know that the road to liberty
Is as long as the road from slavery.

The death of Stephen Lawrence
Has taught us to love each other
And never to take the tedious task
Of waiting for a bus for granted.
Watching his parents watching the cover-up
Begs the question
What are the trading standards here?
Why are we paying for a police force
That will not work for us?

The death of Stephen Lawrence
Has taught us
That we cannot let the illusion of freedom
Endow us with a false sense of security as we walk the streets,
The whole world can now watch
The academics and the super cops
Struggling to define institutionalised racism
As we continue to die in custody

Chapter 2

As we continue emptying our pockets on the pavements,
And we continue to ask ourselves
Why it is so official
That black people are so often killed
Without killers?

We are not talking about war or revenge
We are not talking about hypothetics or possibilities,
We are talking about where we are now
We are talking about how we live now
In dis state
Under dis flag (God Save the Queen),
And God save all those black children who want to grow up
And God save all the brothers and sisters
Who like raving,
Because the death of Stephen Lawrence
Has taught us that racism is easy when
You have friends in high places.
And friends in high places
Have no use whatsoever
When they are not your friends.

Dear Mr Condon
Pop out of Teletubby land,
And visit reality,
Come to an honest place
And get some advice from your neighbours,
Be enlightened by our community,
Neglect your well-paid ignorance
Because
We know who the killers are.

Benjamin Zephaniah

Chapter 2 — Challenge 21

Analysis of techniques used

In order to understand the effectiveness of poetic devices, you need to consider the impact that your choice of words would have on you as a reader. Copy out and complete the boxes below, using words which you believe to be effective in presenting the argument against legalising Euthanasia.

Key moments	Example	Impact on the reader
Emotive language		
Imagery (a picture painted with words)		
Change of speaker		
Use of the senses	*The smell of new mown grass, the scent of flowers*	
Use of rhythm and rhyme		
Use of alliteration	*The smell of new mown grass, the scent of flowers*	
Structure – how is her viewpoints expressed through the order of events in the poem?		

When could I use these skills outside of school?

Chapter 2

> How a reader may respond to this techniques used in this poem
>
> Manning uses a variety of devices to present her powerful views on Euthanasia. Alliteration such as 'music sweet solace for the lonely hours' helps the reader to empathise with the elderly who clearly still have much to live for. Manning subtly and gently uses the senses to create both a vivid and powerful case for allowing life to end naturally. The reader is left with the feeling that it should only be God's decision to call life at an end-no one else's.

Sonnet writing

What is a sonnet?

A sonnet is a type of poem which has particular rules and rhyme scheme. The following sonnet follows the rules of The Shakespeare's sonnet, which has the following rules:

- 14 lines
- each line contains ten syllables
- each line is written in iambic pentameter which a pattern of a non-emphasized syllable followed by an emphasized syllable.
- a rhyme scheme which is ABAB CDCD EFEF GG, in which the last two lines are a rhyming couplet which often sums up the main aspects of the point of view discussed.

In the following sonnet, the debate between living in the town and country is explored. As you read through this, think about how the argument is developed in each line.

The Town Frowns on the Country Clown
Rather be a towny than a farmer?
Then fumigating nostrils is your thing.
Of course – noise pollution makes you calmer.
With sadness then, say laters to bling bling.

Provincial life lacks much in way of cheer.
That buzz, that noise that helps you strut your stuff.
So wonderful to be gripped by that fear.
Those country kids must envy being tough.

So here you are, contentment in denial
With PS3 still lurking from your pack.
Still breeze may sort these notions to a file
Until such time you may have lost that knack.

Food for thought that may cause indigestion
Yet welcome to your mind's decongestion.

Challenge 22

Write your own sonnet on a topical issue in which you argue for and against, using the techniques above.

What has helped me learn effectively today?

Chapter 2

Using scriptwriting as a tool for developing your writing skills

Radio/TV/Film
The key aspects of being an effective scriptwriter are to **show**, not tell. There is not the time to include lots of description, therefore it is the character's actions and their dialogue which should move the story along.

Below are some key elements of story telling which can be applied directly to scriptwriting.

Three Act Structure

First Act	**Exposition** **Locking conflict**	Exposition – show – not tell. Can start with big emotional scene – then come down – yet it shouldn't be bigger than the climax Length of scene in exposition informs the audience of the pace – helps them settle or feel on edge – depending on your purpose. Develop: a) Tone – writer's voice b) Mood – the world created During beginnings, try to create rising tension What is narrative trigger? Could be a death/life changing event or something minor which provokes hidden insecurities/conflicts.
Second Act	**Complications**	Need to find empathy with the character(s). In complications, we need to know jeopardy – what is at stake if the characters do not get what they want?
Third Act	**Climax/ Resolution**	Meet antagonist What gets in the way of your protagonist's wants? Resolution – not always satisfying or sympathetic; it should reflect the overall tone of the narrative.

Chapter 2

Characterisation

Objective → Obstacle → Action → Consequences

- Consider the different needs of your characters and how they may have a similar objective (perhaps survival) yet try to overcome these obstacles/barriers in different ways. Some characters may deal with conflict through confrontation; some may prefer withdraw or escape.
- Main characters have a want – they have hurdles that get in the way
- Need to consider the jeopardy that your characters face – what is at stake? What are they prepared to risk to achieve their objective and overcome their barriers?
- Try to change the journey that your characters have.
- At the end of the story – your main character may run out of time or options which will often lead to the climax

Radio scripts

How do you write a radio script?

Radio scripts are a very complex way of writing that require particular rules in order for it to make sense. It is vital that you put yourself in the mind of the listener (not reader) therefore whenever you change scene or use a prop, this must be signalled to the listener, often by using sound effects. It is also important that your regularly remind the listener where your characters are and **who** they are(without being too obvious!) Also, in many ways, radio uses the most images as you need to constantly create images in the mind of the listener.

Layout and conventions of a radio script

Look through the opening of a radio script on the next page and in groups of 4, allocate the following roles:
Narrator (who reads the directions)
Damian
Jack
May
As you read through this opening think about how the writer informs the actors and the listener of the setting and the characters through the description.

Chapter 2

SCENE 1 INSIDE MOORCROFT FUNERAL DIRECTORS

F/X CLASSICAL MUSIC   *FX sound effects*

DAMIAN   We can turn this rubbish off for a start

F/X RADIO STATION CHANGING TO *I WILL SURVIVE*

DAMIAN   (*singing along badly*)   *Advice to actor on how to play the role*
Kept thinking I could never live without you by my side.
But I spent so many nights, thinking how you did me wrong.

JACK   Can you turn that down? I'm trying to concentrate.

F/X MUSIC VOLUME DECREASES

DAMIAN   Ok, ok bro – though an artist should use music to inspire their work you know

MAY   (*in coffin - lower voice, distant, almost ghostly tone*)
    Directions which informs the listener and actor
Bit more under the eyes wouldn't go a miss love.

JACK   We've got to get this right, otherwise we'll never get another chance, he'll never trust us again.

DAMIAN   Chill out Jack. Dad'll be fine, he's not going to hang around forever.

JACK   If we screw this one up like Mr. Andrews - we're history.

DAMIAN   Mr. Andrews? the fat bloke with the bowel problem?
I left him for half an hour that's all.

JACK   It was over two – you were unprofessional and look at the state he was in.

DAMIAN   I'm sure he got over it.

JACK   Very funny. Pass us the brush.

MAY   Just my luck. The work experience   *Use of pause adds to dramatic tension*
kids without the handcuffs. (PAUSE) Steady! It's not a snowman look-alike contest. Now easy on the lippy. (PAUSE) Bleedin amateurs.

DAMIAN   It's not as if you're auditioning for a beauty contest though are you love?

MAY   Cheeky sod! This is the first facial I've ever had so don't bleedin rush it.
I've been dying for one of these all my life.

JACK   It's got to be spot on. Dad wants to see her and she's staying at the family's house tomorrow night.

MAY   Last thing I need is them all gawping at me

DAMIAN   Bloody Irish! Who'd want to spend the night with a stiff?
Come on bro, I'll help you finish off in the morning

F/X COFFIN SLAMMING SHUT

43

Chapter 2 — Challenge 23

a) Using a well known story/film, write the first scene as a radio script, uing the layout shown.
b) Allocate the parts and ask the rest of the class to listen (without the script) and comment on how much they were able to follow the plan without any visual stimulus.

Writing a TV Script

The conventions for writing a TV script differ from radio in that they are more descriptive and can obviously use images. In pairs read through the following extract from an episode of *Young Dracula*

Episode 1 – WHEN YOU'RE A STRANGER   YOUNG DRACULA
SHOOTING SCRIPT

This episode is set over one day (and one night).
This day is referred to as **DAY 1** and **NIGHT 1** in the scene headers

SCENE 1. EXT. TOWN. DAY 1. 11.54AM
[VLAD (VO)]

    GENTLE CLASSICAL MUSIC, COMPLIMENTING SHOTS
    OF A NORMAL BRITISH TOWN.

VLAD
[VO] All my life I've wanted to fit in, to be ordinary.

                                             CRASH ZOOM TO:

SCENE 1A. EXT. STREET. DAY 1. 11.54AM TIME CONTINUOUS
[VLAD (VO)] [YOUNG GIRLS X 2 (NS)]

    TWO YOUNG GIRLS SKIP HAPPILY TO A BENCH
    OUTSIDE A MODERN GENERAL STORE.

VLAD
[VO] So I thought moving to a new town would be my chance.

    ONE OF THE YOUNG GIRLS TAKES A BIG BITE FROM A SHINY GREEN APPLE.
    THERE'S A LOW OMINOUS RUMBLE IN THE DISTANCE. THE GIRLS TURN.

VLAD
[VO] My chance to be normal.

    OVER THE ROAD'S HORIZON, A BLACK HEARSE APPEARS COMPLETE WITH
    LOADED ROOF-RACK AND BLACKED-OUT WINDOWS. IT GLIDES
    MENACINGLY PAST THE GIRLS, WHO WATCH AGAPE.

VLAD
[VO] But I was forgetting one little thing…

    THE HEARSE PASSES THE GIRLS. THE APPLE ROTS INSTANTLY.
    THE GIRLS SCREAM. THE MUSIC SUDDENLY TAKES A TURN FOR THE MORE
    SINISTER. PICK UP ON HEARSE AND CRASH ZOOM INTO…

                                             CUT TO:

SCENE 1B. INT. HEARSE. DAY 1. 11.55AM TIME CONTINUOUS
[VLAD]

VLAD
[TO CAMERA] I'm a vampire.
    CRASH ZOOM OUT…

What strategies could I use to progress further?

Chapter 2 — Challenge 24

In pairs, write the next scene of this TV script, using the same conventions.

Film scripts

Film scripts offer more opportunity for brief description of character and place which helps the actors and readers to understand the motives of the characters involved. In this script, there is a combination of description and dialogue which helps to create the opening atmosphere. As you read through this, consider how you could use this style of writing to create your own ideas.

NO FLIES ON ME
SCENE 1. EXT. OUTSIDE THE BURKES' HOUSE. FRIDAY. 9PM
Gareth Burke, 13, with curtained hair is playing football with Stuart, also 13, who has spiky red hair, skinny and is constantly looking round his shoulder with uneasy glances as he regular gets fouled and pushed by Gareth as they jostle for the ball. Gareth keeps dribbling past Stuart and shoots into the double gates. Each time he does, he picks up the ball and adds the score to a piece of paper that is on the nearby path.

            STUART
            Ok, ok Gareth you win.

            GARETH
            Just keep playin Stu and stop moaning
            - you can still come back

            STUART
            It's twenty four nil

Gareth stops dribbling around him.

            STUART
            You always win, I can never beat you

            GARETH
            What's up wi you Stu?
              (beat)
            I'll let you win, come on score
            I'll just stand here, promise.

Stuart does not find this too appealing and looks even more dejected by the offer. He is about to reply when the boys' attention is alerted by the sound of a door opening. Gareth looks towards his house and sees the door ajar. He kicks the ball deliberately at Stuart so it ricochets off him and hits the gate.

            GARETH
            See. You've got one back already
            Tomorrow yeh?

GARETH'S POV: We see Stuart forcing a smile back towards Gareth

            STUART
            Seizure!

Both boys pretend they are having a fit before going in separate directions. As Gareth walks down his path towards the open door, he spots some ants scuttling towards the lamppost. He tries to stamp on them but they escape just in time through a crack in the paving

            GARETH
            There's always tomorrow my little friends.

In what other subjects could I apply these skills?

Chapter 2

As Gareth walks towards the door that has been left ajar by his mum, he notices a fly trapped in a web created by arch of the light and lamppost. Gareth watches it struggle as a spider goes towards it. As he gets towards his house he avoids the lines of cracked slates and pushes the door open.

CUT TO:

SCENE 2. INT. THE GROVE PUB. FRIDAY 9.05PM
A pint glass can be seen, just visible in a smoky, run-down catholic club. An oldish man, about fifty, begins drinking the guiness slowly; around him we notice that almost every table seats a single man in the same position. Another man holds his pint up slowly – Jimmy Burke returns the drunken salute. He is now looking through the fog of smoke at the clock behind the bar – but it's difficult to see the time through the smoke.

SMOKE DISSOLVES TO:

SCENE 3. INT. BURKES' HOUSE. FRIDAY. LIVING ROOM. 9.10PM
The smoke now begins to clear and we see a clock (above a chipped stone fireplace) We realise it's Gareth who is trying to make out the time. He looks towards the figure slumped on the settee. It is his mum, Teresa, who is in her mid-forties, naturally attractive yet who clearly neglects herself, shown through the tattered hair, frayed nightgown and ripped slippers. She is asleep with her lit cigarette in one hand and cheap martini in the other. We see Gareth's point of view as he sees his mum's head above the brown settee. Gareth now acts in a ritual way: turns the TV off and the fire, stubs out the cigarette that his mum is still holding, turns off the light and picks up a grey, heavy overcoat from the hallway and leaves the house.

CUT TO:

SCENE 4. INT. THE GROVE PUB. FRIDAY. 9.30PM
The same grey heavy overcoat is being put on Jimmy by his son and the landlord. Jimmy has clearly been asleep but begins to awaken due to his son's arrival.

      JIMMY
    How's is going son?
    Is your mam ok?

      GARETH
    She's fine dad, let's go home.

      JIMMY
    How about one for the road son?

      LANDLORD
    Come on Jimmy, this lad should be in bed b'now

      JIMMY
    You're a good lad son, aren't you?
    Lookin after your old man.
      (beat)
    Your mam, have you checked?

      GARETH
      (methodically)
    Fire's out,
    cig out,
    lights off.
    Can we go home dad?

Chapter 2

Future Skills

You are interested in becoming a scriptwriter and decide to adapt the following extract (from Eveline) into **one** of the following formats:

- Radio
- TV
- Film

Use the skills developed in this unit to adapt this scene.

She stood among the swaying crowd in the station at the North Wall. He held her hand and she knew that he was speaking to her, saying something about the passage over and over again. The station was full of soldiers with brown baggages. Through the wide doors of the sheds she caught a glimpse of the black mass of the boat, lying in beside the quay wall, with illumined portholes.

She felt her cheek pale and cold and, out of a maze of distress, she prayed to God to direct her, to show her what was her duty. The boat blew a long mournful whistle into the mist. If she went, tomorrow she would be on the sea with Frank, steaming towards Buenos Aires. Their passage had been booked. Could she still draw back after all he had done for her? Her distress awoke a nausea in her body and she kept moving her lips in silent fervent prayer.

A bell clanged upon her heart. She felt him seize her hand: `Come!'
All the seas of the world tumbled about her heart. He was drawing her into them: he would drown her. She gripped with both hands at the iron railing. `Come!'

No! No! No! It was impossible. Her hands clutched the iron in frenzy. Amid the seas she sent a cry of anguish. `Eveline! Evvy!'

He rushed beyond the barrier and called to her to follow. He was shouted at to go on, but he still called to her. She set her white face to him, passive, like a helpless animal. Her eyes gave him no sign of love or farewell or recognition.

Chapter 2

Personalised Progression
Assessment Focus 1: write imaginative, interesting and thoughtful texts

How is my work at KS3 assessed?

Your work is assessed using assessment focuses which help you and your teacher determine on what level your work is currently at. This criteria is often used when assessing your APP work and other classroom assessments. In this unit we will be looking at how to progress in AF1 (see above)

Key questions:

- What level am I currently working at in this assessment focus for writing? (if unsure, ask your English teacher)
- What skills do I currently have in this assessment focus?
- What skills do I need to develop to get to the next level?

In this section, you will be completing a series of challenges which will show you how you can personally progress to the next level, using many of the skills that you have developed in this unit.

How can I practice my skills to reach the next level in this assessment focus?

- Consider what excites you when you read or watch something.
- What is it that captures your attention?
- Think of a character that you identify with. What is it about the way they have been created which engages you in their dilemmas/struggles and achievements?
- Experiment with using some of the literary techniques (such as use of adverbs/adjectives/similes/metaphor)
- Use different voices in your writing; you could be an optimist/cynic.
- When writing about character, remember the ingredients needed to make them believable.
- Consider plot from the point of view of how your main character(s) try to reach their goal by overcoming barriers in their way.
- Remember the difference between narrator (storyteller) and author (you)
- As the author, you can manipulate the characters so that they reveal your own personal viewpoints. (Use them as a vehicle).
- In non-fiction, ensure that every word and presentational feature that you employ has a role in impacting on your audience and helping you to achieve your purpose.
- Use a combination of description, narration and dialogue to engage your reader.
- Use subtly and ambiguity to draw your reader in.
- Good drama is created when the audience feels enveloped with the jeopardy that the characters face.

Chapter 2

- Be consistent in your tone of writing and tense, unless it is used in a controlled way for a particular effect.
- Find a range of fiction and non-fiction and judge how effective you think they are in impacting on you (and the intended audience)

In this assessment focus (AF1), if you are currently working at…

Level 3	go to Progress Checker A (Level 3-4 progression)
Level 4	go to Progress Checker B (Level 4-5 progression)
Level 5	go to Progress Checker C (Level 5-6 progression)
Level 6	go to Progress Checker D (Level 6-7 progression)

When you get to the stage where you feel that you are confident in a particular level in this assessment focus, you can attempt the challenges for the next level.

Chapter 2

Progress Checker A (Level 3-4 progression)

	Assessment Focus 1 – write imaginative, interesting and thoughtful texts	
1	What level am I currently working at in AF1 writing?	Level 3
2	What skills do I currently have in this assessment focus?	As a Level 3 writer in AF1 I am able to: • include some appropriate ideas and content; • provide some detail on the basic information and events that I describe • occasionally take on a specific viewpoint (role) when writing
3	What skills do I need to develop to reach the next level?	To be a confident AF1 writer at Level 4 I need to: • choose relevant ideas and content • develop some ideas and material in detail • establish and maintain a straight forward viewpoint

AF1 Progress Challenge

Moving a Level 3 response to Level 4

1) The table below includes a Level 3 response in AF1. Look at how this pupil has achieved this level and think about what they could do to improve.

Describe a place that filled you with fear.

AF1 – Level 3 response	Why the pupils achieved at Level 3
I was scared at the graveyard and there were horrible sounds from the church and I was thinking about the city match and whether my mate could come.	*Viewpoint is occasionally maintained (of a frightened person) though loses focus (referring to city match)* *Graveyard is an appropriate place for a frightening experience.* *The event is described using the adjective 'horrible'*

Chapter 2

How could we move this response into Level 4?

AF1 – Level 3 response	AF1 – Level 4 response
I was scared at the graveyard and there were horrible sounds from the church and I was thinking about the city match and whether my mate could come.	*I was scared at the graveyard, ==which was just past my old primary school== and there were horrible sounds from the church which made me think ==about all those horror films I shouldn't have watched as a kid==*

Notice how the Level 4 response
- Uses relevant ideas and content (graveyard/reference to horror film)
- Some ideas developed in detail (just past school)
- Viewpoint/role maintained (rather than mentioning city match, this pupil links the feelings of fear with horror films)

Read through the next paragraph from the Level 3 response and improve the quality, using the advice given above.

The leaves were rumbling and it was really dark so I decided to try and ring my friend though my mobile had no credit, I wish I had got it sorted out though I ran out of time because I had footie.

Next steps…

a) Look at a piece of written work you have completed recently. Remind yourself of the task and highlight it in two colours:
1) relevant parts 2) irrelevant

Change/remove the irrelevant parts, depending on what you need to do.

b) Check carefully what **role** you have been asked to take on as a writer and consider what particular **viewpoint** they would have on a particular topic. In the example above one of the main reasons why the second pupil achieved a level 4 rather than a level 3 is because they maintained a consistent viewpoint (i.e. someone scared) rather than mentioning irrelevant things like a football match and mobile phone credit.

Chapter 2

Progress Checker B (Level 4-5 progression)

	Assessment Focus 1 – write imaginative, interesting and thoughtful texts	
1	What level am I currently working at in AF1 writing?	Level 4
2	What skills do I currently have in this assessment focus?	As a Level 4 writer in AF1 I am able to: • choose relevant ideas and content • develop some ideas and material in detail • establish and maintain a straight forward viewpoint
3	What skills do I need to develop to reach the next level?	To be a confident AF1 writer at Level 5 I need to: • use imaginative detail • shape my ideas into the appropriate form • maintain clear viewpoint and include some elaboration

AF1 Progress Challenge

Moving a Level 4 response to Level 5

The table below includes a Level 4 response in AF1. Look at how this pupil has achieved this level and think about what they could do to improve.

AF1 – Level 4 response	Why the pupils achieved at Level 4
I was scared at the graveyard, which was just past my old primary school and there were horrible sounds from the church which made me think about all those horror films I shouldn't have watched as a kid	• Uses relevant ideas and content (graveyard/reference to horror film) • Some ideas developed in detail (just past school) • Viewpoint/role maintained as this pupil links the feelings of fear with horror films)

Chapter 2

How could we move this response into Level 5?

AF1 – Level 4 response	AF1 – Level 4 response
I was scared at the graveyard, which was just past my old primary school and there were horrible sounds from the church which made me think about all those horror films I shouldn't have watched as a kid	I was **terrified approaching the graveyard, not just because of the thick fog which blurred my view.** It was just past my old primary school, **a pretty haunting place itself,** and there were horrible sounds **echoing** from the church.

Notice how the Level 5 response
- Uses imaginative detail: use of the verb 'terrified' rather than the more predictable choice of 'scared'; extra detail regarding the fog;
- Clear viewpoint established with development of individual voice (interesting extra comment about primary school)

Next steps…
- When writing descriptively, think about what extra imaginative detail would make your writing more interesting.
- Remember that any extra detail should add to the effect you want to create on your reader.
- Be very clear on your persona (the role you have been asked to take on as a writer) and think about the following how they would:

a) sound
b) get excited about
c) feel anxious about
d) get their message across

- When writing your first draft, use double space so you can add interesting detail.

Chapter 2

Progress Checker C (Level 5-6 progression

Assessment Focus 1 – write imaginative, interesting and thoughtful texts	
1 What level am I currently working at in AF1 writing?	Level 5
2 What skills do I currently have in this assessment focus?	As a Level 5 writer in AF1 I am able to: • use imaginative detail • shape my ideas into the appropriate form • maintain clear viewpoint and include some elaboration
3 What skills do I need to develop to reach the next level?	To be a confident AF1 writer at Level 6 I need to: • imaginatively use appropriate materials and writing conventions • adapt writing style to suit purpose and audience • establish an individual voice or point of view that is mostly sustained throughout • vary the level of formality used for purpose and audience • use a range of stylistic devices used to achieve effects

Chapter 2

AF1 Progress Challenge

Moving a Level 5 response to Level 6

The table includes a Level 5 response in AF1. Look at how this pupil has achieved this level and think about what they could do to improve.

Task set: Write a letter of complaint about a recent holiday you have been on.

AF1 – Level 5 response	Why the pupils achieved at Level 5
Not only did our shower not work (you needed one after being squashed in that broken lift for half an hour!) the bath was covered in grime.	• uses imaginative detail (extra section about the lift) • maintains clear viewpoint and include some elaboration (viewpoint/voice is assertive and sarcastic, which you would expect when writing a complaint)

AF1 – Level 5 response	AF1 – Level 6 response
Not only did our shower not work (you needed one after being squashed in that broken lift for half an hour!) the bath was covered in grime.	*I know we were probably asking too much when we said we wanted running water in a four star hotel. Not only did your excuse for a shower not work (you needed one after being squashed in that broken lift for half an hour!) the grime in the bath became good friends with the cockroaches.*

Notice how the Level 6 response
- is more imaginative in its use of details i.e. sarcasm (asking too much of four star hotel)
- more cutting in its tone (excuse of a shower) which suits the purpose and audience
- has a more authoritative tone, through the extended use of sarcasm (became friends with cockroaches)

Next steps…
- Research the persona's role that you are asked to take on.
- For each paragraph of writing you produce, write a one line reply from your target audience.
- Is it achieving the effect you intended?

Chapter 2

Progress Checker D (Level 6-7 progression

	Assessment Focus 1 – write imaginative, interesting and thoughtful texts	
1	What level am I currently working at in AF1 writing?	Level 6
2	What skills do I currently have in this assessment focus?	As a Level 6 writer in AF1 I am able to: • imaginatively use appropriate materials and writing convention • adapt writing style to suit purpose and audience • establish an individual voice or point of view that is mostly sustained throughout • vary the level of formality used for purpose and audience • use a range of stylistic devices used to achieve effects
3	What skills do I need to develop to reach the next level?	To be a confident AF1 writer at Level 7 I need to: • successful adapt of wide range of forms and conventions to suit a variety of purposes and audiences • establish and sustain a distinctive individual voice or point of view • control the level of formality and vary my use of stylistic devices to achieve intended effect

Chapter 2

AF1 Progress Challenge

Moving a Level 6 response to Level 7

The table below includes a Level 6 response in AF1. Look at how this pupil has achieved this level and think about what they could do to improve.

AF1 – Level 6 response	Why the pupils achieved at Level 6
Dear Ms. Pinter, *We write to you about a Venezia push chair and car seat that we bought from you recently. First of all I need to let you know what happened to begin with:* *We have attempted to use this product for the last three months yet it has been impossible to use, causing my daughter Annabelle to get upset after the broken handlebar which is why we have written this letter. Read below please which explains why we require our money back* *Wheels are rickety. I asked about the wheels when choosing a pram and was told that they would be ok to handle walks etc. However, we have found the pram extremely unsteady and dangerous.*	• Familiar with conventions of how to write a letter of complaint. (clear opening and structured argument developed) • Convincing tone sustained with examples of formal language used for effect.

Chapter 2

How could we move this response into Level 7?

AF1 – Level 6 response	AF1 – Level 7 response
Dear Ms. Pinter, We write to you about a Venezia push chair and car seat that we bought from you recently. First of all I need to let you know what happened to begin with: We have attempted to use this product for the last three months yet it has been impossible to use, causing my daughter Annabelle to get upset after the broken handlebar which is why we have written this letter. Read below please which explains why we require our money back Wheels are rickety. I asked about the wheels when choosing a pram and was told that they would be ok to handle walks etc. However, we have found the pram extremely unsteady and dangerous.	Dear Ms. Pinter, We write to you ==further to our recent communications regarding== the Venezia pushchair and car seat that we ==purchased== from you recently. Firstly, ==a reminder of the key points from our initial complaint:== We have attempted to ==persevere== with this product for the last three months yet it has been ==increasingly== impossible to use, ==causing great discomfort== to ourselves and baby Annabelle; eventually this has ==culminated== in its broken handlebar, hence this letter. The following bullet points are a summary of our concerns and highlight ==why we require== an alternative pushchair or a refund: Wheels are rickety. I ==specifically== asked about the wheels when choosing a pram and was ==informed== that they would be sturdy enough to handle walks etc; however, we have found the pram extremely unsteady and dangerous, ==creating the feeling of little control when steering or going over uneven ground.==

Notice how the Level 7 response:
- Controls the formal tone through its consistent use of standard English and sophisticated vocabulary used for effect
- Uses imaginative detail which supports the overall point of view expressed.
- Distinctive voice is sustained throughout in order to impact directly on the target audience which would lead to a greater chance of achieving its purpose

Chapter 2

Next steps…

1) Produce a vocabulary bank of formal and informal words; i.e.:
   bought – purchased
   got – received
   collected - accumulated

2) Make a list of all the possible target audiences that you might need to consider before writing.

3) Produce a specific bank of formal/informal words that would be suitable for that specific audience

4) When writing imaginatively, remember to refer to other texts/situations in order to support your viewpoint and further increase your chances of impacting on your target audience and achieving your purpose.

5) Place your writing persona in different contexts in order to get a greater sense of how they should most effectively communicate.

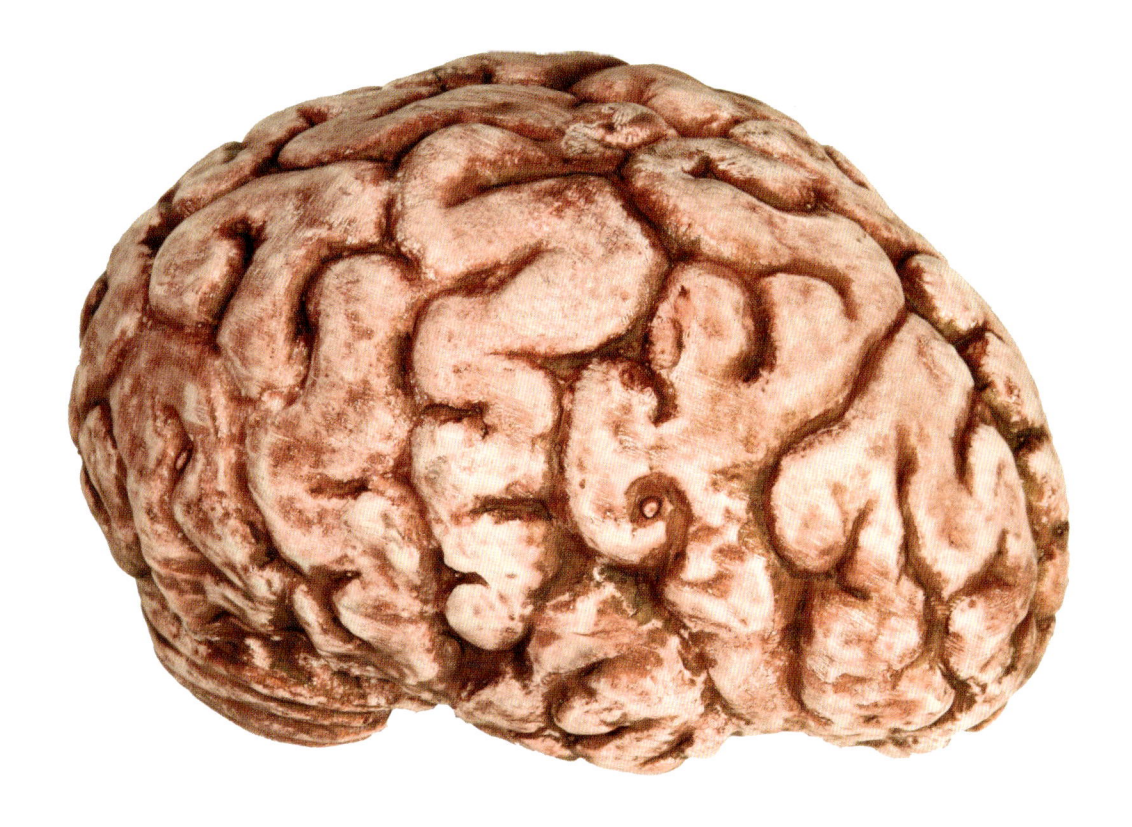

Chapter 3 — This time it's personal

Programme of Study Links	**Competence** - being clear, coherent and accurate in written communication
Framework Objectives	**8.2** varying sentences and punctuation for clarity and effect **9.1** using conventions of standard English **9.2** using grammar accurately and appropriately **10.2** commenting on language use
Personal Learning & Thinking Skills	Creative thinkers Reflective learners
AFL	Peer-assessment Exploration of success criteria
Assessment Focus	AF5 – write sentences for clarity, purpose and effect AF6 – write with technical accuracy of syntax and punctuation in phrases, clauses and sentences
Functional Skills	Using correct grammar, punctuation and spelling Producing writing for purposes and contexts beyond the classroom.

Challenge 1 - Get thinking

a) Write a paragraph on what you watched on TV last night, using the punctuation marks on your right.

b) In pairs, discuss what these words might mean
- argy-bargy
- bang out of order
- belly up
- bend someone's ear
- big girl's blouse
- on yer bike
- keep your hair on
- ker-ching
- kushty
- lager-lout
- living in la-la land
- lead up the garden path

.
?
,
!
'
…
-
( )
;
:

When could I use these skills outside of school?

Chapter 3

In this unit I will learn how to effectively…
(Learning Objectives)

- vary sentences and punctuation for clarity and effect
- use the conventions of standard English
- use grammar accurately and appropriately
- comment on how language is used

The topics I will be studying are…
(Stimulus)

- Diary/biography and autobiography
- Letter writing
- Blogging and text

My understand will be checked by seeing how I…
(Assessment Criteria)

- (AF5) write sentences for clarity, purpose and effect
- (AF6) write with technical accuracy of syntax and punctuation in phrases, clauses and sentences

My achievement will be demonstrated through me successfully completing the following challenges:
(Learning Outcomes)

Challenge	1	Get thinking – punctuation & slang analysis
Challenge	2	Changing meaning of sentences
Challenge	3	Sentence experiment (group task)
Challenge	4	Using punctuation effectively.
Challenge	5	Punctuation peer assessment.
Challenge	6	Analysis of sentence use
Challenge	7	Personal writing reflection
Challenge	8	Rewriting speech
Challenge	9	Using slang for dramatic effect
Challenge	10	Letter of complaint
Challenge	11	Developing formality
Challenge	12	Blogging
Challenge	13	Creative texting

Future skills
Formal letter advice

Chapter 3

What type of sentences are there?

statement	question	command	exclamations
We could go for a meal after the film finishes.	Why do you want me to go home	Go past the shop on the left and you will find the post box there.	What a waste of a life!

What do we mean by sentence structure?

SIMPLE SENTENCE: a sentence containing one clause (it does not have to be short in length though should only have one **clause**

A clause is a group of words that express an event

I stood in the rain.

COMPOUND SENTENCE: a sentence with two or more clauses joined by a coordinating conjunction; each clause are of equal weight (importance) and are both main clauses.

I stood in the rain screaming whilst the ambulance sped off down the drive

COMPLEX SENTENCE: a sentence with a **main clause** and a **subordinating clause**

I stood in the rain which was dripping down my face.

A main clause makes sense on its own and can form a complete sentence. i.e: **It was freezing** A subordinate clause is part of the main clause and cannot make sense on its own. i.e. He went to bed (main clause) because he was tired (subordinate clause)

Why is it important to vary sentence types and length?

From the point of view of your reader, it is important that the type of sentences that you use reflect the meaning you are trying to get across. This can be achieved in a number of ways:

Vary the way sentences begin:

What different effects are created?

Simon felt cold and lonely and went back to bed.
To Lonely and cold, Simon went back to bed.
Or The bed awaited Simon as he was cold and lonely.

Using short sentences to emphasis a point:
Why should I put up with it? Drugs are for losers.

Chapter 3 — Challenge 2

Rewrite the following sentences through changing the word order

James was feeling upset because he got into trouble at school and was frightened of his mum coming home to find out.

Use complex sentences to add extra detail and interest.

Look at the example below which has been taken from the original sentence of *Simon felt cold and lonely*.

> Simon, the frail teenager who still lived with that dark secret, shivered ferociously in the church, like a prisoner awaiting execution. Loneliness he was used to, but this sight which lay in front of him, was something that even his father hadn't prepared him for.

- **Indicates personality and age**
- **Use of a dramatic simile**
- **Hints at disturbing past**
- **Alliteration/use of the senses**
- **Vague description 'sight' to engage reader's curiosity and create suspense**
- **Gives background details**

The simple idea of cold and lonely has been used with great effect here to demonstrate how you can extend simple sentences in order to make your writing more lively and entertaining for the reader.

Short sentences can also be used for dramatic effect, especially when used alongside longer, more complex sentences.

> He awoke from that blissful sleep, with soothing memories caressing his thoughts. His eyes opened with great anticipation of the day's events. Then something began to trouble him. The bed felt damp. Blood oozed through his fingers. Not again! Not so soon.

- **Long, complex sentence used to create a feeling of calm and tranquillity**
- **Short, powerful sentences used to reflect the change of mood from peacefulness to anxiety.**

What has helped me learn effectively today?

Chapter 3 — Challenge 3

What strategies could I use to progress further?

In a learning group of 3, experiment with using the following techniques to extend and improve your sentences and the quality of your writing:

Tools	Examples From…	To…
Using ing verbs to begin a sentence	I left the graveyard, shivering and shaking with fear	**Shivering** and **shaking**, I left the graveyard
Using ed verbs to begin a sentence	John climbed the wall, filled with fear	**Filled** with fear, John climbed the wall
Begin a sentence with an adverb	Rachel walked along the canal bank nervously	**Nervously**, Rachel walked along the canal bank
Beginning sentences with prepositions	The bag lay abandoned and forgotten under the floorboards	**Under** the floorboards, the bank lay abandoned
Begin sentences with an expanded noun phrase (power of 3)	The air made my skin crawl	The **cold**, **clean**, **crisp** air made my skin crawl
Use simple sentences for effect	When I went into the garage, after being out for the afternoon, I found him dead.	**I found him dead in the garage**
Use compound sentences to add detail	The Jennings family had their little girl.	The Jennings family had their little girl **and they believed she was a gift from God**.
Use complex sentences to add interest to the sentence	I lie to my parents all the time.	I lie to my parents all the time **because I am scared of them realising the truth about me**.
Use short sentences for emphasis/to create tension	I doubt that anyone in our party would survive this weather	**No one would survive.**
Use of contrasting sentence lengths for effect	Evidence clearly shows that there is a huge increased risk to you having a heart attack if you keep smoking. If this doesn't make you want to give up, nothing will.	Evidence clearly shows that there is a huge increased risk to you having a heart attack if you keep smoking. **Still dying for a fag?**

Chapter 3

Autobiography/Biography/Diary

What's the difference?

An **autobiography** is a life story individually written by that person. (usually in first person)

A **biography** is a life story of someone else's life. (third person)

A **diary** is a personal reflection of someone's thoughts and feelings which does not have the initial intention to be shared with someone else.

However, the term 'diary' seems to have become more public in recent years with many celebrities/sport stars/politicians using a diary to record their personal thoughts and feelings though with every intention of publishing it at a later date.

The following diary entry (although obviously published later) is from the point of view of a former smoker who describes the journey to give up smoking. As you read and begin analysing the text, consider how the writer varies his sentence structure to express his thoughts and feelings.

- Awareness of target audience (smokers who need help with quitting)
- Practical advice
- Emotional advice
- Feelings of trying to give up
- Rewards of winning the battle.
- Powerful use of language
- Informative language
- Persuasive language

Here's How I Quit Smoking

I tried to quit smoking so many times I lost count. Almost every day for several years I promised myself that I wouldn't light up that first cigarette of the day. My parents smoked and I started smoking to "fit in" with my friends at school.

I wanted to quit smoking so badly but I knew in my heart that I just enjoyed smoking too much! I was aware of all the dangers of smoking knowing full well that continuing to smoke would eventually have a major impact upon my health. There can't be a smoker out there who isn't aware of the dangers and risks of smoking. With all of the news in the last several years about the dangers of smoking and the impact of second hand smoke, it amazes me that teen smoking and women smoking rates are on the increase.

Chapter 3

Wanting desperately to quit smoking, one day I woke up and made a promise to myself (and my 3 year old son!) that I wouldn't smoke for the whole day no matter what happened. Miraculously I managed to go the day without lighting up and I was soon into my second day of not smoking. Before I knew it I had made it a whole week.

I was really proud of my personal accomplishment and I let everyone know about it! I was completely over the physical addiction within 5 days. I would be lying if I told you that it was easy. I was irritable, had difficulty concentrating and sleeping but I made it through the first stage of quitting.

The most difficult part to overcome was the social, psychological addiction. This, by the way, is the part that most people have trouble with and is one of the main reasons for relapses and what many smokers give as the reason for not wanting to quit smoking in the first place.
It isn't easy but if you set your mind to it and not give into the urges you will find that you can learn how to cope more and more as each day passes. Quitting smoking is a learning process. I know several ex-smokers that quit several years ago and still have the occasional urges (me being one of them!). I also know many smokers who will never quit because they can't get overcome this social/psychological addiction. I am living proof that you CAN quit smoking if you put your mind to it.

I devised a coping mechanism that I still use whenever I get the urge for a cigarette:

visualize the black hot stinky tar laden smoke scalding my oesophagus as it makes its way down to my now clean pink healthy lungs that are now healing from the many years of abuse that I put them through!

Winning The Battle...

When I quit smoking (the last and final time), I knew I would be tested many times to see if I could make it in the world of non-smokers. The ultimate test was coming up at my mother's annual Christmas family get-together. Spending the long cold Canadian winter months in Florida, she always has a family dinner just before they depart south. Out of the fifty people that attend, about 25 of them smoke. I knew that this was going to be my "big" test as a non-smoker.

Chapter 3

I had been thinking about this gathering for at least a week and I had some apprehensions about whether I would make it through it and come out still smoke-free. All of the normal cues for wanting and having a cigarette were there for me. You know - the drinking, family members, good food, discussions about everything and anything.

The best advice that I can give to someone who is trying to quit smoking is to take it one day at a time, remember that it gets better with each passing day, and that the health benefits are worth every bit of effort that goes into the quitting process.

Time Heals...
Let me tell you how I feel now that I have quit smoking and how I think that I've changed since I quit. I am sure that there are a lot of you out there who can identify with most of these items:

I feel more in control of my actions and a lot of people have told me that they think that I'm surer of myself and more in control. Before, if I had a problem at work, I would go outside and have a smoke and hope that it would go away on its own. Now I seem to be able to confront the problem and solve it without having to hide behind something. I actually find that I enjoy challenging problems at work as I take delight in the fact that I feel confident enough in my ability to win out. I also find when I deal with my employees that I am more positive and sure of myself. They seem to notice this and a few of them have told me that they like this change. Maybe I am giving them more direction, something they were not getting before.

I find that I have a lot more patience. I used to blow up quite easily before at work and at home. My wife used to say that I was "like a stick of dynamite ready to blow up." I was like that at work as well. I feel at lot calmer now. I find that I am not rushing everything I do. I take the time. The University where I work should be happy because they are getting more work out of me. I am much more productive and the work that I do is getting better.

I am now at the point where I can honestly say, without a word of doubt, that I do feel better. Like I said earlier, not a lot better, but enough that I don't want to start up again. For all of you less than a month smoke-free'ers, give it time and you shall see that the benefits of not smoking are overwhelming. You will start to feel better every day you stay off cigarettes, and true to fashion, the old saying "Time heals," will prevail.

Chapter 3

How effective sentence structures and punctuation are used effectively (1 of 2)

My parents smoked and I started smoking to "fit in" with my friends at school.	Effective use of quotation to add realism
I wanted to quit smoking so badly but I knew in my heart that I just enjoyed smoking too much!	Realistic and honest tone and use of exclamation mark identifies with the reader.
There can't be a smoker out there who isn't aware of the dangers and risks of smoking	Uses exclamations well to reveal how foolish he feels about himself for not giving up sooner.
Wanting desperately to quit smoking, one day I woke up and made a promise to myself (and my 3 year old son!) that I wouldn't smoke.	Fronted clause used powerfully to increased the reader's anticipation of what his views are. Use of brackets and apostrophe adds interest and detail to his reflections.
Miraculously I managed to go the day without lighting up and I was soon into my second day of not smoking the whole day no matter what happened.	Powerful adverb enhances the modest tone displayed and draws the reader into his story.
I would be lying if I told you that it was easy	Simple, short sentence adds emphasis to his recount.
I was irritable, had difficulty concentrating and sleeping, but I made it through the first stage of quitting.	Use of subordination adds interesting detail to reveal state of mind. Power of 3 used powerfully to reveal 'journey made': 1) irritable 2) difficulty concentrating and sleeping 3) made it
This, by the way, is the part that most people have trouble with and is one of the main reasons for relapses and what many smokers give as the reason for not wanting to quit smoking in the first place	Variety in sentence structures helps to connect the ideas to the reader. Use of commas to highlight the phrase 'by the way' helps the reader identify with the challenges in giving up smoking
It isn't easy but if you set your mind to it and not give into the urges you will find that you can learn how to cope more and more as each day passes. Quitting smoking is a learning process	Direct appeal to the reader 'you' Variety in sentence length and types, adds emphasis to point of view expressed.

Chapter 3

How effective sentence structures and punctuation are used effectively (2 of 2)

I know several ex-smokers that quit several years ago and still have the occasional urges (me being one of them!).	Use of brackets reinforces the idea that he is able to identity with the struggles even though he has personally triumphed.
I am living proof that you CAN quit smoking if you put your mind to it.	Use of imperative sentence and capital use adds to uplifting and positive tone.
I visualize the black hot stinky tar laden smoke scalding my oesophagus as it makes its way down to my now clean pink healthy lungs that are now healing from the many years of abuse that I put them through!	Exaggerated use of adjectives used to reinforce the disgusting effects of smoking. Juxtaposition of the way his lungs used to be and how they are now
When I quit smoking (the last and final time)	Optimistic tone emphasised through the use of brackets.
You know - the drinking, family members, good food, discussions about everything and anything	Personalised language 'you' as well as effective punctuation (the dash and commas) to organise and clarify the range of points made.
Before, if I had a problem at work, I would go outside and have a smoke and hope that it would go away on its own. Now I seem to be able to confront the problem and solve it without having to hide behind something.	Effective use of adverbs to highlight the journey made.
My wife used to say that I was "like a stick of dynamite ready to blow up." I was like that at work as well. I feel at lot calmer now. I find that I am not rushing everything I do. I take the time.	Use of direct speech creates greater realism. List of shorter, simple sentences adds to the sense of closure.
I am now at the point where I can honestly say, without a word of doubt, that I do feel better.	Effective use of subordination adds greater emphasis to points being made.
You will start to feel better every day you stay off cigarettes, and true to fashion, the old saying "Time heals," will prevail.	Final sentence encapsulates the tone of optimism and reassurance

Chapter 3 — Challenge 4

In what other subjects could I apply these skills?

Using punctuation effectively.

Choose an occasion that sticks in your memory – something that has had a big impact on you. Produce a couple of paragraphs which includes all of the punctuation below.

.	Full stops to indicate when a sentence is finished
?	Question to indicate when a question is being asked (either literal or rhetorical)
,	Use of commas to • separate items in a list • to mark off for extra information (Simon, my boss, was nowhere to be found.) • to separate clauses in a sentence (Despite the rain, we enjoyed the match) • to organise where connectives are used (However, this did not dampen our spirits)
!	Exclamation mark to express a particular emotion (Don't over use otherwise it loses its effect.)
'	Use of apostrophe to indicate where letters have been omitted. I am (I'm) or to indicate possession (my friend's party) Remember if it is plural and already ends in 's' then the apostrophe comes after the 's' (the boys' toilet)
' '	Quotation marks to indicate direct speech
...	Use of ellipses for dramatic effect…
-	Use of dash to separate ideas clearly
( )	Use of brackets to add extra information and emphasise an idea.
;	Semi-colon to separate two closely linked sentences
:	Colon to introduce a list or to expand the meaning of a sentence (It was boiling hot: over one hundred degrees.)

Chapter 3 — Challenge 5

Peer assess

Swap each other's paragraphs and highlight where each punctuation mark was used. Make two positive comments about how the punctuation has been used and make one suggestion of how it could be improved.

Read through the following extract which has been adapted and simplified from Clive James' autobiography. Consider how the sentence structures and punctuation could be improved to make his experiences come alive for the reader.

> I could not build go-carts very well. Other children made superb carts with wooden frames and wheels that screamed on the pavements like a diving aeroplane. The best I could manage was a fruit box with silent rubber wheels taken off an old pram.
>
> After school and at weekends boys came from all over town to race along our street. There would be twenty or thirty carts. The noise was incredible.
> Go-carts racing down the pavement on one side had a straight run of about a quarter of a mile all the way to the park. The carts would reach such high speeds that it was impossible for the rider to get off. All he could do was crash when he got to the end.
>
> On the other side of the road we could only go half as far, before a sharp right-angle turn into Irene Street. The back wheels slid round the corner, leaving black, smoking trails of burnt rubber, or skidded in a shower of sparks.
>
> The Irene Street corner was made more dangerous by Mrs Braithwaite's poppies. Mrs Braithwaite lived in the house on the corner. We all thought that she was a witch. We believed that she poisoned cats. She was also a keen gardener. Her flower beds held the area's best collection of poppies. She had been known to phone the police if even one of her poppies was picked by a passer-by.

When could I use these skills outside of school?

Chapter 3

It was vital to make the turn into Irene Street without hurting a single poppy, otherwise the old lady would probably come out shooting. Usually, when the poppies were in bloom, nobody dared make the turn. I did because I thought that I was skilful enough to make the turn safely.

But I got too confident. One Saturday afternoon I organised the slower carts like my own into a train. Every cart was loosely bolted to the cart in front. The whole thing was twelve carts long, with a big box cart at the back.

I was in my cart at the front. Behind me there were two or three kids in every cart until you got to the big box cart, which was crammed full of little kids, some of them so small they were sucking dummies.

Why did I ever suggest that we should try the Irene Street turn? With so much weight the super-cart started slowly, but it sped up like a piano falling out of a window. Long before we reached the turn, I realised that I had made a big mistake. It was too late to do anything except pray. Leaning into the turn, I slid my own cart safely around in the usual way. The next few carts followed me, but each cart was swinging out ever more widely. Out of my control, the monster lashed its enormous tail.

The air was full of flying ball-bearings, bits of wood, big kids, little kids and dummies. Most terrible of all, it was also full of poppy petals. Not one flower escaped. Those of us who could still run scattered to the winds, dragging the wounded kids with us. The police spent hours visiting all the parents in the district, warning them that the carting days were definitely over.

Text: **From Unreliable Memoirs**
by **Clive James, Macmillan UK**

Chapter 3 — Challenge 6

Analysis of sentence use

I could not build go-carts very well.

a) This simple sentence (with one clause) is an effective opening as it quickly sets the comic tone. Change this sentence into a complex one to make the tone more serious. You may wish to add punctuation.
For example

> "I could not build go-carts very well - or friendships"

b) Improve the final sentence in the paragraph below to add extra detail; use some of the tools we have looked at earlier.

> **After school and at weekends boys came from all over town to race along our street. There would be twenty or thirty carts. The noise was incredible.**

c) How has Clive James used commas effectively in the following sentence?

The back wheels slid round the corner, leaving black, smoking trails of burnt rubber, or skidded in a shower of sparks.

c) Using the same sentence structure, describe an exciting occasion that you have been on (real or make believe) Include the following:

- Adjective
- Verb
- Adverb
- Variety of punctuation

d) The following paragraph has too many simple, short sentences. Experiment by including some compound and complex sentences, using a range of adjectives and adverbs.

> **Mrs Braithwaite lived in the house on the corner. We all thought that she was a witch. We believed that she poisoned cats. She was also a keen gardener. Her flower beds held the area's best collection of poppies. She had been known to phone the police if even one of her poppies was picked by a passer-by.**

What has helped me learn effectively today?

Chapter 3

The following sentence is effective in using the fronted clause (Out of my control) and the use of metaphor to describe the go cart (monster).

Out of my control, the monster lashed its enormous tail.

e) Using this sentence structure, describe a dangerous situation you have found yourself in (real or make-believe)
For example,

Screaming for air, I finally escaped from the pool.

f) The following sentence uses commas effectively to separate the action.

The air was full of flying ball-bearings, bits of wood, big kids, little kids and dummies.

Using the same dangerous situation you described earlier, replicate this use of commas in which you describe the disaster.

g) Replicate the sentence structure below to include an effective description of your dangerous situation.
For example:

**Most terrible of all, it was also full of poppy petals.
Not one flower escaped.**

Most................................, it was...

Not one ....

Writing from the heart

When writing a diary entry/biography about someone you care about, particularly if they have passed away, it is very difficult to get the correct tone, especially if you wish to write for yourself as well as for a reader. Being over emotional in your writing can often miss-communicate what you want to say, though you also want to express your emotions with passion and conviction so that your reader gets a real sense of the person you are writing about, and your feelings towards them.

The following extract from Jillian Morgan gives a moving account of her mum's final days before she passed away. As you read through this, consider how the writer manages to express her feelings with powerful emotion yet is still able to communicate her ideas effectively with her reader.

Chapter 3

Kathryn

She felt torn as she was about to reach the biggest transitional period of her life - into another existence. As always mum's mainconcerns were related to other people and their feelings. She had spent the last two years desperately trying to find acure for this deadly disease and through experimenting with every potion and alternative treatment going she had prolonged herlife considerably and inspired many.
At this moment in her lifeand on a personal level she was physically and mentallyexhausted and ready to go.

"You're the main reason that's stopping me from going you know!" she said, while gripping tightly of my hand and staring fearfully into my eyes.

I was a little taken back and didn't quite know what to say. Throughout my whole life my mum always expected me to tell the truth and I wasn't going to let her down now. My eyes started to well up and my heart started to pound because I knew this was the point where I was going to have to let go and release her.

"The truth is, I can't bear the thought of you not being here anymore and still feel like I need you. But I love you more than anything in the world and I can't stand to see you suffering anymore. I just want you to be at peace. I need to let you go."

My heart was breaking, and mum's was splitting too. That bond, that closeness we shared was, and still remains, unbreakable; therefore the pain of eternal separation was sole destroying forus both. The strongest emotion of all was love, which was guiding me and enabling me to let go.

"You are my little girl and I never ever wanted to leave you, butI know that you will find your own happiness and I will be watching over you, sharing with you those happy moments.Whenever you need me I will be right by your side." As we held each other tight, no more words were needed, as there was amutual understanding of what was to come.

That night mum went to sleep, still holding my hand and drifted into her new life with tentative expectancy. Love can be the happiest feeling in the world but can also be the most painful, especially when that feeling never dies.

By Jillian Morgan

Chapter 3

Example from text	Methods use to communicate emotionally and clearly to the reader
She felt torn as she was about to reach the biggest transitional period of her life - into another existence.	Personification to evoke the image of being ripped apart. Effective use of dash – to make the link explicit.
She had spent the last two years desperately trying to find a cure for this deadly disease	Alliteration used to reveal the frustration felt
"You're the main reason that's stopping me from going you know!" she said, while gripping tightly of my hand and staring fearfully into my eyes.	Use of direct speech to enhance the realism Adverb used "fearfully" to effectively describe the emotions
My eyes started to well up and my heart started to pound because I knew this was the point where I was going to have to let go and release her.	Description of emotional and physical response
My heart was breaking, and my mum's was splitting too.	Use of compound sentence to reveal the equal suffering
That bond, that closeness we shared was, and still remains, unbreakable; therefore the pain of eternal separation was sole destroying for us both.	Commas and semi-colon used powerfully to organise the range of feelings expressed
That night mum went to sleep, still holding my hand and drifted into her new life with tentative expectancy.	Use of adjective 'tentative' and abstract noun 'expectancy' effectively communicates the depth of emotions felt.

Chapter 3 — Challenge 7

How can I apply these skills for my own writing?

Choose somebody that you are close to and practice using these techniques to describe them powerfully

- Personification to evoke the image of..
- Effective use of dash – to make the link explicit.
- Use of adjectives and abstract nouns to communicate …
- Alliteration used to reveal…
- Commas and semi-colon used powerfully organise the range of feelings expressed
- Use of direct speech to enhance realism
- Use of compound sentence to reveal …
- Adverbs used to effectively describe the emotions

Someone who is close to me

What strategies could I use to progress further?

Adapting writing style to suit your audience

Writing an effective:

- letter
- blog
- text

With the ever increasing use of email, mobile phones and text messages you probably think the days of letter writing are long gone. Wrong! – Try applying for a college place or new job by text message - you won't have much luck.

In this section we will be looking at:

- the different types of written communication;
- the particular features of each one;
- how to adapt your tone to achieve your purpose;
- how to impact effectively on your target audience.

77

Chapter 3

Standard English is the very formal aspect of English that is held by many to be 'correct' or 'accepted' way of communicating that is not influenced or affected by different variations in regional dialect

Dialect is the variety of language that is spoken by a group in a particular area or of a social group. It can have a different accent (and pronunciation), vocabulary and use different grammatical structures.

A person's **accent** is the way he or she speaks, with differences in the sounds that can show the place a person comes from

Slang is language at its most informal, which can be described as non-standard and ungrammatical. It is often used within small social groups and can be considered offensive in some cases.

Colloquial language is informal language (everyday) that would not be used in formal situations.

It is also important that to use the passive voice effectively; for example:

It is also important that you use passive voice; for example:

Passive voice	Active voice
The election was won by Obama who gained a greater number of votes than McCain.	Obama won the election. (or) McCain lost the election

Even though both statements are true, the passive voice presents the election result as being done to Obama and McCain whereas the active voice description personalises the victory (Obama won) as well as the defeat (McCain lost)

Challenge 8

Changing the meaning through the use of passive voice

Your friend gives you the following speech which he/she has written in response to losing the student council leader election. You need to rewrite this so that the responsibility does not seem your friends – he was a victim of circumstances.

I have lost this election because I did not listen to the needs of students and should have focused more on trying to improve our school. My poor attendance meant that I was unable to attend the meeting regularly enough and I will so everything I can to win your trust back in the hope of representing you again in the future.

In what other subjects could I apply these skills?

Chapter 3 — Challenge 9

Using slang for dramatic effect

Read through the text below which is from a government crime safety leaflet and rewrite this, using the A-Z of slang words on the following page to change the meaning. You could perhaps write it from the point of view of the criminal or a victim.

Personal Safety

The chances that you or a member of your family will be a victim of violent crime is low. Violent crimes are still comparatively rare and account for a very small part of recorded crime. Nevertheless, many people are frightened that they, or someone close to them, will be the victim of a violent attack.

Walk facing the traffic so a car cannot pull up behind you.

The best way to minimise the risk of attack is by taking sensible precautions. Most people already do this as part of their everyday lives, often without realising it. You may already be aware of some of the suggestions listed below, but some may be new to you, and you may find them useful. They may seem particularly relevant to women, but if you are a man, don't stop reading or turn the page. You can act positively to contribute towards women's safety, as well as reducing the risk of assault on yourself.

How can you stay safe?

At home

Make sure your house or flat is secure. Always secure outside doors. If you have to use a key, keep it nearby - you may need to get out quickly in the event of fire.

If other people such as previous tenants could still have keys that fit, change the locks. Don't give keys to workmen or tradesmen, as they can easily make copies.

If you wake to hear the sound of an intruder, only you can decide how best to handle the situation. You may want to lie quietly to avoid attracting attention to yourself, in the hope that they will leave. Or you may feel more confident if you switch on the lights and make a lot of noise by moving about. Even if you're on your own, call out loudly to an imaginary companion – most burglars will flee empty-handed rather than risk a confrontation. Ring the police as soon as it's safe for you to do so. A telephone extension in your bedroom will make you feel more secure as it allows you to call the police immediately, without alerting the intruder.

When could I use these skills outside of school?

Chapter 3

A-Z of slang

argy-bargy	cough up	jack all	quids in
adam and Eve	crank up	karsy	rabbit in a
bananas	cushy number	keep your hair	head light
bang out of	dead cert	on	random
order	deffo	ker-ching	rattled
beach bum	diamond	kushty	readies
belly up	geezer	lager-lout	rip-off
belt up	ear bashing	la-la land	rocket science
bend	elbow grease	lead up the	round the
someone's ear	egg on your	garden path	bend/houses/
big girl's	face	lose the plot	twist
blouse	fag	mad for it	shell out
on yer bike	flake out	magic sponge	sorted
do one	float your	maccy D's	summat
billy no mates	boat	make it snappy	take a chill pill
bits and bobs	gabbing	mardy	throw a
bling bling	glad-rags	make	wobbly
blow a fuse	hairy moment	mincemeat of	two-ticks
blow the	half-cut	someone	up the swanny
whistle	handbags	muck in	up for it
bodge job	happy as larry	naffed off	unhinged
booze	heebie jeebies	narked off	vibe
bottle it	hissy fit	needle	wadded
brassed off	hunky dory	nice one	waffle
bung	hyper	off your	walking
buzzin	innit	trolley	disaster
caned it	in the dog	old banger	xray eyes
chav	house	pants	yap
cheesed off	iron out	pig-headed	yob
chill out	jam packed	pull a fast one	zonked

Chapter 3

How to make your writing more formal

It is possible to be more formal in your use of language using the following techniques:

Increased formality

	From	To
Using more sophisticated vocabulary	It may seem The action began The ambulance guy helped. I went without saying bye	It may appear The action commenced The paramedic assisted… I departed without saying goodbye
Removing unnecessary colloquial expressions (more suited to speech)	I was sort of thinking of maybe going to the match	I was considering attending the match
Change from first person to third person	I cannot believe we can't vote at 16	Sixteen year olds should be able to vote.
Changing two verbs to one	Smoking less will cut down your chance of heart disease I had to put up with the stink of her fags	Smoking less will reduce your chance of heart disease I had to endure the putrid smell of her cigarettes
Change adjectives to abstract nouns	It was a stupid decision which cost him his job.	It was an act of stupidity which cost him his job.
Removing informal abbreviations	You mustn't smoke whilst pregnant	You must not smoke whilst pregnant
Using more sophisticated connectives	So Next In the end	Therefore Subsequently Finally
Moving from active voice to passive voice	We decided to tell the police.	The police were informed of our concerns

Chapter 3

Communicating effectively through letter writing

Letter writing is not about rules or regulations and should be concerned with getting your message across in a suitable way to satisfy both your purpose and audience.

Writing a letter of persuasion

The example below demonstrates how to write in a controlled and assertive way, without having a threatening and aggressive tone. It has been written in response to the purchase of a pram from *'Mummys and Daddys.'* The writer is very unhappy with the purchase and the subsequent problems that has been created. As you read through this letter consider what methods are used to make the argument clear, whilst also having a persuasive tone.

Mr & Mrs. Moran
8 Main Road
Moss Side
Manchester
M20 9RX
0161 2861767
07789000615
2morans@heyyou.co.uk

April 16th 2009

Ms. Pinter
Sales Manager
Mummys and Daddies
Unit 99
Cheshire Village Outlet
Cheshire
CH4 7TL

Re: purchase of Venezia pushchair – purchased on 21 February 2009

Dear Ms. Pinter,

We write to you regarding the above pushchair and car seat that we purchased from you recently. Firstly, a reminder of the key points from our initial complaint:
We have attempted to persevere with this product for the last three months yet it has been increasingly impossible to use, causing great discomfort to ourselves and baby Annabelle; eventually this has culminated in its broken handlebar, hence this letter. The following bullet points are a summary of our concerns and highlight why we require an alternative pushchair or a refund:

- Wheels are rickety. I specifically asked about the wheels when choosing a pram and was informed that they would be sturdy enough to handle walks etc. However, we have found the pram extremely unsteady and dangerous, unbalanced and having the feeling of little control when steering or going over uneven ground.
- The steering of this pushchair feels like a damaged shopping trolley as the wheels seem to have a life of their own. We have carefully compared our vehicle with other prams and there is a general agreement that the pushchair lacks any sense of control or direction I its movement.
- When attempting to push the trolley our legs constantly bang into the foot bar, causing discomfort.
- It is also very low compared to other pushchairs, resulting in backache and restricted movement.

Chapter 3

- There are many gaps in the sides of the pushchair (when back into a pram style) which results in a cold draft coming through to our baby.
- Car seat – the baby is cramped in the car seat; her head slumps forward and then it swings about when going round corners because of the shape and poor design of the seat. In addition, the buttons on either side of the seat are extremely stiff and very difficult to use.
- The sun canopy is clumsy, with no suitable place to store it.
- The maternity bag we purchased is far too big to place under the small storage available under the pram. The bag regularly get stuck and there is no room for additional materials, such at baby blankets, etc.

Since this letter was sent to you, our disappointment and dissatisfaction with your service has deepened, due to the following points:

1. The temporary replacement pushchair that we received smells of smoke and has stains on it throughout. This is a huge concern due to the high risk of cot death for babies under 6 months. This has caused a great deal of stress and concern to ourselves as new parents.
2. We were not given a replacement (temporary) sun canopy which has been extremely difficult to cope with in view of the time of year (hot summer months) Our baby has been at serious risk every time we have gone out in the sun. Consequently, we have been forced to stay in doors during this time for the safety of our baby – resulting in her being neglected of fresh air.
3. No replacement rain cover was given, which again has caused much disruption during the rainy days.
4. We were told by Colette (Manager) that no refund or replacement car seat would be considered yet we have since been made aware that a customer (Andrew) who actually happened to go into Mamas and Papas at the same time as us, has been given a full cash refund. He had the same issue as ourselves, namely the fact that its design forces our baby daughter's head to lurch forward, potentially causing neck ache. We have compared our car seat and Andrews with other models and it is clear that there is a problem with the design. Why has there been a cash refund for one customer when we were told that was not an option for ourselves? We have been in contact with Andrew who is more than happy to support our case if need be.
5. Having already spend a great deal of time and money (petrol costs) driving from Manchester to Cheshire Oaks, we have since been told that we need to bring the replacement pram back – costing us extra money and time.
6. We have been informed that no refund or replacement will be given; therefore we have been forced to purchase another pram as we are seriously concerned about the safety of our child, for the reasons listed above.

We chose Mamas and Papas because of its reputation and good name, therefore we have been very disappointed with the advice given to us, and the consequent problems that we have incurred. This has caused a great deal of distress during our first few months of parenthood with our first child and in spite of our best efforts, we have had a very disappointing response to our justifiable complaint.

We have been forced to take this matter further. Please find enclosed letter sent to Watchdog, Office of Fair Trading, National Consumer's Council. I have also emailed this letter to Radio 5 Live who are currently discussing this issue of consumer dissatisfaction. We hope that in view of all of the above that a full cash refund can be returned to ourselves for both the pram and the car seat.

Yours sincerely,
Mr & Mrs Moran

Chapter 3

Analysing the persuasive devices.

Copy the table below and record the persuasive methods used by Mr & Mrs. Moran. An example has been completed for you.

Polite/ Formal tone	We write to you regarding the above pushchair and car seat that we purchased from you recently.
Opinions disguised as facts	Wheels are rickety.
Personal examples	We have compared our car seat and Andrews' with other models and it is clear that there is a problem with the design.
Use of emotive language…	causing great discomfort to ourselves and baby Annabelle.
Being assertive	The following bullet points are a summary of our concerns and highlight why we require an alternative pushchair or a refund:
Compliments given for dramatic effect	We chose Mamas and Papas because of its reputation and good name.

Challenge 10

Consider an occasion that you have been disappointed with something – it could be the quality of a game you have bought; a piece of clothing you have had; or a meal you have eaten. Using the techniques explored above, write this letter, ensuring that you are assertive – not aggressive in your tone.

Chapter 3 — Challenge 11

Developing formality

Your friend wants some advice on how to write a formal letter of application and sends you the application letter below. You need to:
a) read the letter and add/delete where appropriate
b) text him (only use a maximum of 10 words – abbreviations are ok too) some advice.

> Hiya,
>
> I'm John and i love newspapers, especially the sun – its G8t. any chance of some work at your place – I only liv down the road and m dad, well, not m real dad, though, you know what I mean, he goes to work and sed he cud drop me off.
>
> So far, I mus have read loads of papers – man united is my favrite team – though I live in dublin can I write about them when I get the job?
>
> I know its suppose to be work experience though wud you pay us if I right really well?
>
> Please text us to let me know wen I can start Buster – the mosha rules.

Using email/ blogs and text

Informal language that informs and entertains

Using email and text as a form of communication is ever more popular, mainly due to the accessibility, speed and low cost, compared to letter writing; however, due to the sheer volume of emails that we send and receive, quite often, personal emails can get lost in the middle; there is also the argument that the process of writing a letter, putting in an envelope, placing on the stamp and physically going to the postbox or post office attached more importance to the communication made; moreover, physically receiving a letter through the post, particularly if it is of personal value can have more impact than the process of pressing a few buttons on a mobile or computer.

If you are feeling angry with someone the process of sending a quick text or email can often be a disadvantage as there is no time to reflect on what you have said before it has been sent. The process involved in writing a letter can often give you time to cool down before it's too late!

Me,me,me,me,me!

Using Blogging

Increasingly, the internet has allowed individuals to create virtual network of friends (instant messenger/facebook/bebo/twitter) as well as publish our own thoughts on the world through the use of blogging which is basically an on-line diary which shares an individual's thoughts and feelings to a potential world wide audience. In video sharing sites such as **You Tube** we are able to upload footage that we feel others would like to enjoy.

Blogging is generally written in an informal way, using colloquial language and slang, that is personal to the writer as well as entertaining for the reader.

What strategies could I use to progress further?

Chapter 3

The following blog by Mark Boardman is a collection of his thoughts on
- Big Brother
- DIY
- X-factor
- More DIY
- Exam results
- Stomach bug
- Music concert
- yellowblogroad.com

As you read through this blog, consider how colloquial language is used to inform and entertain the reader.

The Yellow Blog Road
so the end of bb and this last week then

Hardly seems a week since the BB final. At least The Law Of The Playground is back though, which pleased Lisa.

The BB final panned out as predicted, with Pete winning of course. For many weeks I'd pictured that scene with Pete and Glyn the only two people left in the house, and it was pretty much as I'd imagined. The only disappointment was Pete's interview, but I guess he was always going to be unable to speak. His main aim was to "sort my mum out", but at the back of his mind must have been some notion of publicising Tourette's. I have to confess that I changed my opinion on that during the series. At the start I thought that people would laugh at him for the wrong reasons. Guess I was wrong.

Saturday I spent finishing the bathroom windowsill and door for political reasons. Also realised from the radio that X Factor was starting that night. Here we go again. Quite amusing in the event though, and looks like Trevor is making a comeback.

Sunday. Usual round of shopping and stuff. Some revelations about Cornwall that went surprisingly well.

Monday saw some flurrying about door handles, and then it was time to get Gemma and Kane from the airport. Again, it all went smoothly, and I needn't have worried – although I couldn't help it.

Tuesday and Wednesday were committed to some DIY in Clitheroe. I think it went well, in the end, although a supposedly simple plumbing job turned into a nightmare, largely because of the unorthodox methods of the previous occupant. Compression joints on plastic barrier pipe. Phase to neutral reversal – sounds like a job for the Enterprise. Some rumbling in the pipes.

Thursday was GCSE results day. I really struggled with whether to go in or not, but in the end decided I might as well put myself out my misery. Brigid had also said, from her roof terrace in Holland, that she wouldn't mind her own SAT and GCSE results. I was really pleasantly surprised with the results for my own GCSE group. I suppose really intelligent students are bound to do well.

Friday and Saturday I had hoped to finish the bulk of my paper, but I was struck by some weird stomach thing that robbed me of energy. Spent most of Saturday in bed. Today I'm kind of returning to normal. Saw most of a storming set by Muse at Reading before bed last night.

Chapter 3

The Yellow Blog Road	*Adapted use of the culturally well known 'The Yellow Brick Road' to colloquially describe the 'journey' made that week.*
so the end of bb and this last week then	*Informal sentence beginning – expressed in colloquial dialect form.*
Hardly seems a week since the BB final. At least The Law Of The Playground is back though, which pleased Lisa.	*Use of informal adverb 'hardly'.*
The BB final panned out as predicted, with Pete winning of course. For many weeks I'd pictured that scene with Pete and Glyn the only two people left in the house, and it was pretty much as I'd imagined. The only disappointment was Pete's interview, but I guess he was always going to be unable to speak. His main aim was to "sort my my mum out", but at the back of his mind must have been some notion of publicising Tourette's.	*Colloquial tone 'pretty much' 'I guess'.* *Use of direct speech.* *Comment on wider implications.*
I have to confess that I changed my opinion on that during the series. At the start I thought that people would laugh at him for the wrong reasons. Guess I was wrong.	*Change in sentence type and length - reflects change in viewpoint.*
Saturday I spent finishing the bathroom windowsill and door for political reasons. Also realised from the radio that X Factor was starting that night. Here we go again. Quite amusing in the event though, and looks like Trevor is making a comeback.	*Interesting use of adjective 'political' which subtly suggests some marital pressure on doing the housework.*
Sunday. Usual round of shopping and stuff. Some revelations about Cornwall that went surprisingly well.	*One word sentence (without adverb/adjective hints at mundaneness of the day. Use of colloquial phrase 'and stuff' adds to informal tone and the dismissive description of 'Sunday'.*
Monday saw some flurrying about door handles, and then it was time to get Gemma and Kane from the airport. Again, it all went smoothly, and I needn't have worried – although I couldn't help it.	*Effective verb 'flurrying' juxtaposed effectively with 'door handles' which creates the comic effect.*

Chapter 3

Tuesday and Wednesday were committed to ==some DIY in Clitheroe==. I think it went well, in the end, although a supposedly simple plumbing job turned into a nightmare, largely because of the unorthodox methods of the previous occupant. ==Compression joints on plastic barrier pipe. Phase to neutral reversal – sounds like a job for the Enterprise.== Some rumbling in the pipes.	*Colloquial phrase 'some DIY in Clitheroe* *Intentionally includes too much (plumbing) detail so that the tone can be brought back to the light-hearted 'Enterprise' comment, punctuated effectively with the dash.*
Thursday was GCSE results day. I really struggled with whether to go in or not, but in the end decided I might as well put myself out my misery. Brigid had also said, from her roof terrace in Holland, that she wouldn't mind her own SAT and GCSE results. I was ==really pleasantly== surprised with the results for my own GCSE group. I suppose really intelligent students are bound to do well.	*Use of adverb 'pleasantly' is further intensified with 'really' to reveal genuine sense of unexpected achievement.*
Friday and Saturday I had hoped to finish the bulk of my paper, but I was struck ==by some weird== stomach thing that ==robbed== me of energy. Spent most of Saturday in bed. Today I'm ==kind of== returning to normal. ==Saw== most of a ==storming set== by Muse at Reading before bed last night.	*Colloquial use of language* *Effective use of alliteration*

The Yellow Blog Road is an effective way of capturing an individual's week in an informal and entertaining way. Notice how the sentence structure, punctuation and colloquial language choices contribute to the meaning wanting to be communicated.

Challenge 12

Applying the techniques

Using these techniques, write your own blog – it could be a description of a week or a particular event that has had an impact on you.

In what other subjects could I apply these skills?

Chapter 3

Challenge 13

How can texting develop me as a writer?

Any form of communication that you are involved in can only help you as a writer, particular as you are learning how to adapt your style of writing to suit your audience. When you write texts, there is a general expectancy that you will be more concise (straight to the point) which are skills often needed in more extended pieces of writing.

cuL8r

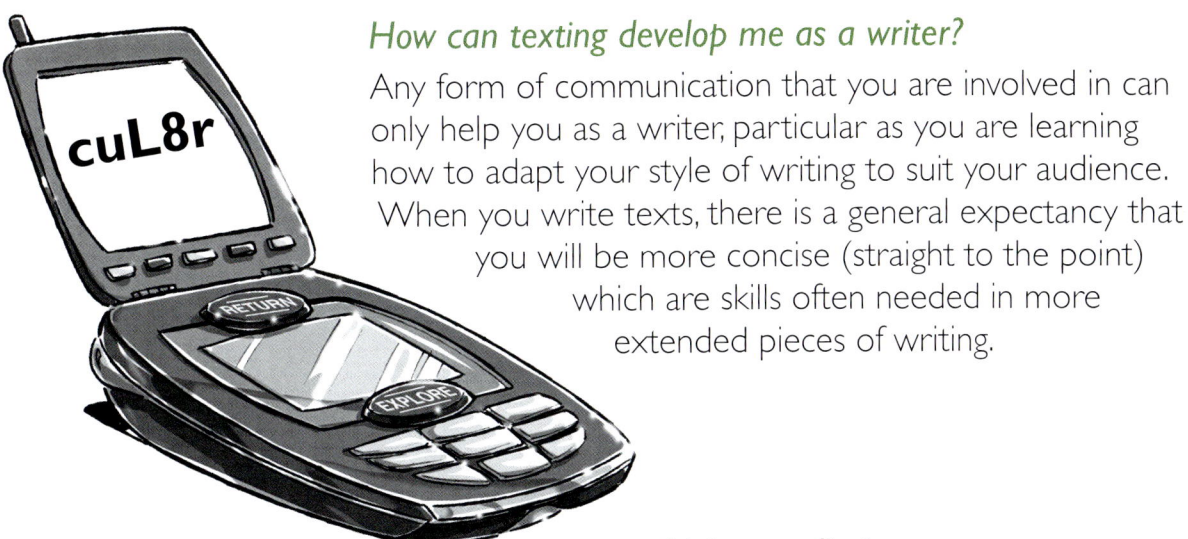

Using predictive text

The advantage of using predictive text is that it can help you with your spelling (it tries to guess what word you are formulating) and it also gives you vocabulary choices.

There are also interesting and unexpected links between words that arise when you try and use predictive text. For example:

More/Nose/Nope
See/Red/Ref/Pee
Hope/Gore/Hose/Gord
Jon/Loo
Mark/Mask
Lazy/Jazz

- Type in a variety of words about yourself (using your blog) and practice using predictive text. What is the effect of the word change?
- Shorten your blog into one text message, selecting and editing your blog carefully.
- Text your friend an opening for a short story who needs to add a sentence and forward it on to someone else (you could change the genre of the writing every time it changes.

Future skills

Your school is hoping to become a Specialist Sports College and your headteacher has asked you to write a letter to the Secretary of State for Education in support of your school's bid. It is important that you communicate your ideas clearly, whilst explaining why your school, and the local community would benefit from being a Specialist Sports College.

When could I use these skills outside of school?

Chapter 3

Personalised Progression
Assessment Focus 5 – vary sentences for clarity, purpose and effect

How is my work at KS3 assessed?

Your work is assessed using assessment focuses which help you and your teacher determine on what level your work is currently at. This criteria is often used when assessing your APP work and other classroom assessments. In this unit we will be looking at how to progress in AF5 (see above)

Key questions:

- What level am I currently working at in this assessment focus for writing? (if unsure, ask your English teacher)
- What skills do I currently have in this assessment focus?
- What skills do I need to develop to get to the next level?

In this section, you will be completing a series of challenges which will show you how you can personally progress to the next level, using many of the skills that you have developed in this unit.

How can I practice my skills to reach the next level in this assessment focus?

In this assessment focus (AF5), if you are currently working at…

Level 3	go to Progress Checker A (Level 3-4 progression)
Level 4	go to Progress Checker B (Level 4-5 progression)
Level 5	go to Progress Checker C (Level 5-6 progression)
Level 6	go to Progress Checker D (Level 6-7 progression)

When you get to the stage where you feel that you are confident in a particular level in this assessment focus, you can attempt the challenges for the next level.

Chapter 3

Progress Checker A (Level 3-4 progression)

	Assessment Focus 5 – vary sentences for clarity, purpose and effect	
1	What level am I currently working at in AF5 writing?	Level 3
2	What skills do I currently have in this assessment focus?	As a Level 3 writer in AF5 I am able to: • mainly use simple sentences; • use connectives such as: *and, but so*; • sometimes vary my tenses and verb forms.
3	What skills do I need to develop to reach the next level?	To be a confident AF5 writer at Level 4 I need to • attempt to vary the length, structure and subject of sentences; • use some subordinating connectives, e.g. *if, when* and *because*; • vary my tense and verb forms.

AF5 Progress Challenge

Moving a Level 3 response to Level 4

1) The table below includes a Level 3 response in AF5. Look at how this pupil has achieved this level and think about what they could do to improve.

Task: Discuss the arguments for and against legalising Euthanasia (assisted death for terminally ill patients) in Britain.

AF5 – Level 3 response	Why the pupil achieved a Level 3
Euthanasia is wrong. You might not really want to die. Euthanasia is ok if you are in loads of pain.	• Uses simple sentence structure • Uses simple connectives 'and' and 'as'

How could we move this response into Level 4?

AF5 – Level 3 response	AF5 – Level 4 response
Euthanasia is wrong. You might not really want to die. Euthanasia is ok if you are in loads of pain.	==Some people== think Euthanasia is wrong ==because== you don't get the chance to change your mind ==whereas others have said== that you should be allowed to get rid of pain if you are going to die anyway. ==There is no right answer.==

Chapter 3

Notice how the Level 4 response
- Varies sentence length and structure
- Subordinating connectives used (because/whereas)
- Variation in tense form (others have said)

Next steps…
- Highlight your work for when you use simple connectives such as and, but, so. Could you use a subordinate connective instead?
- Vary your sentence structure and length to try and achieve different effects.
- In discursive writing (where a topic is debated) make sure that you plan your arguments clearly, choosing the right connective to either add a point or compare/contrast opinions in your writing.

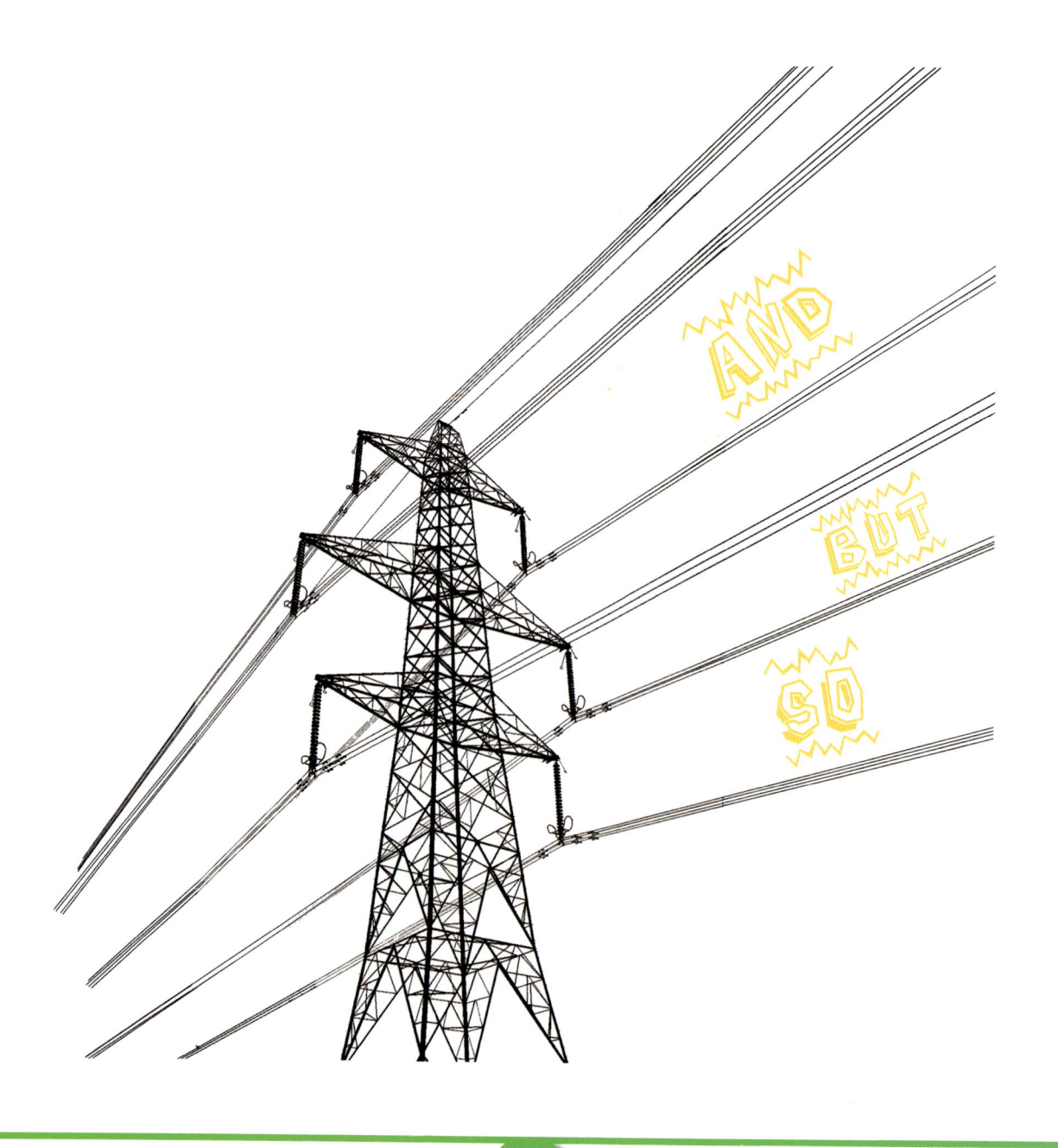

Chapter 3

Progress Checker B (Level 4-5 progression)

Assessment Focus 5 – vary sentences for clarity, purpose and effect	
1 What level am I currently working at in AF5 writing?	Level 4
2 What skills do I currently have in this assessment focus?	As a Level 4 writer in AF5 I am able to • attempt to vary the length, structure and subject of sentences; • use some subordinating connectives, e.g. *if, when* and *because*; • vary my tense and verb forms.
3 What skills do I need to develop to reach the next level?	To be a confident AF5 reader at Level 5 I need to • vary my sentence lengths, structures and subjects to provide clarity and emphasis; • use a wide range of connectives to clarify relationship between ideas; • use some features of sentence structure to build up detail or convey shades of meaning.

AF5 Progress Challenge

Moving a Level 4 response to Level 5

The table below includes a Level 4 response in AF5. Look at how this pupil has achieved this level and think about what they could do to improve.

AF5 – Level 4 response	Why the pupil achieved a Level 4
Some people think Euthanasia is wrong because you don't get the chance to change your mind whereas others have said that you should be allowed to get rid of pain if you are going to die anyway. There is no right answer.	• Varies sentence length and structure • Uses subordinating connectives used (because/whereas) • Varies his use of tense form (others have said)

Chapter 3

How could we move this response into Level 5?

AF5 – Level 4 response	AF5 – Level 5 response
Some people think Euthanasia is wrong because you don't get the chance to change your mind whereas others have said that you should be allowed to get rid of pain if you are going to die anyway. There is no right answer.	Some people think Euthanasia is wrong because you don't get the chance to change your mind; ==clearly, this is a powerful argument. Others rightly argue== that you should have a choice about ending your life, ==particularly if you are in terrible pain.==

Notice how the Level 5 response
- Varies sentence structure for effect
- Uses a wider range of connectives
- Sentence structure is created to add to the meaning intending to be put across.

it would seem	on the strength of	possibly
one might consider suggest	to the best of one's belief	maybe
propose/deduce/infer	theoretically	contrary to
presumably	literally	improbably
in the view of	obviously	incredibly

Next steps…

Opinion and interpretation

- Use more sophisticated connectives when making your opinion clear
- Vary sentence lengths and structures to help make your points clearer

Chapter 3 **Challenge 13**

Progress Checker C (Level 5-6 progression)

	Assessment Focus 5 – vary sentences for clarity, purpose and effect	
1	What level am I currently working at in AF5 writing?	Level 5
2	What skills do I currently have in this assessment focus?	As a Level 5 writer in AF5 I am able to • vary my sentence lengths, structures and subjects to provide clarity and emphasis; • use a wide range of connectives to clarify relationship between ideas; • use some features of sentence structure to build up detail or convey shades of meaning.
3	What skills do I need to develop to reach the next level?	To be a confident AF5 writer at Level 6 I need to • use of a variety of simple and complex sentences to achieve purpose and contribute to overall effect; • confidently use of a range of sentence features to clarify or emphasise meaning.

What has helped me learn effectively today?

AF5 Progress Challenge

Moving a Level 5 response to Level 6

The table below includes a Level 5 response in AF5. Look at how this pupil has achieved this level and think about what they could do to improve.

AF5 – Level 5 response	**Why the pupil achieved a Level 5**
Some people think Euthanasia is wrong because you don't get the chance to change your mind; clearly, this is a powerful argument. Others rightly argue that you should have a choice about ending your life, particularly if you are in terrible pain.	• Varies sentence structure for effect • Uses a wide range of connectives • Sentence structure is created to add to the meaning intending to be put across.

95

Chapter 3 — **Challenge 14**

How could we move this response into Level 6

AF5 – Level 5 response	AF5 – Level 6 response
Some people think Euthanasia is wrong because you don't get the chance to change your mind; clearly, this is a powerful argument. Others rightly argue that you should have a choice about ending your life, particularly if you are in terrible pain.	*Some people, ==particularly those who may have had personal involvement with the issue==, argue that Euthanasia should still be outlawed because the patient is often not in the correct frame of mind to make such a huge decision. ==This may be true==, though this is a tiny percentage of people, ==argue those who want a change in the law==.*

What strategies could I use to progress further?

Notice how the Level 6 response

- Controls the variation in sentence structure for effect (to help develop the discussion)
- Confidently uses these sentence structures to add relevant detail and manage the debate in a considered way.

Next steps…

- Practice beginning sentences with a verb, particularly 'ing' verbs. Running/Screaming/Beating etc
- Begin sentences with an adverb to grab your reader's attention: Frantically… Nervously…
- Check through your work and make sure there is a variety of simple, complex and compound sentences.

Chapter 3

	Assessment Focus 5 – vary sentences for clarity, purpose and effect	
1	What level am I currently working at in AF5 writing?	Level 6
2	What skills do I currently have in this assessment focus?	As a Level 6 writer in AF5 I am able to: • use a variety of simple and complex sentences to achieve purpose and contribute to overall effect; • confidently use of a range of sentence features to clarify or emphasise meaning
3	What skills do I need to develop to reach the next level?	To be a confident AF5 writer at Level 7 I need to • thoughtfully use a variety of sentence types across the text to achieve purpose and overall effect; • shape sentences that have individual merit and contribute to overall development of the text.

AF5 Progress Challenge

Moving a Level 6 response to Level 7

The table below includes a Level 6 response in AF5. Look at how this pupil has achieved this level and think about what they could do to improve.

AF5 – Level 6 response	Why the pupils achieved a Level 6
Some people, particularly those who may have had personal involvement with the issue, argue that Euthanasia should still be outlawed because the patient is often not in the correct frame of mind to make such a huge decision. This may be true, though this is a tiny percentage of people, argue those who want a change in the law.	• *Controls the variation in sentence structure for effect (to help develop the discussion)* • *Confidently uses these sentence structures to add relevant detail and manage the debate in a considered way.*

Chapter 3

Progress Checker D (Level 6-7 progression)

How could we move this response into Level 7?

AF5 – Level 6 response	AF5 – Level 7 response
Some people, particularly those who may have had personal involvement with the issue, argue that Euthanasia should still be outlawed because the patient is often not in the correct frame of mind to make such a huge decision. This may be true, though this is a tiny percentage of people, argue those who want a change in the law.	==Easy-death clinics.== Book your mum for a morning appointment and you can sort out the funeral arrangements in the afternoon. ==What could be easier?== This is the view held by pro-life groups who claim that legalising Euthanasia will make a mockery of life itself. ==Try telling that== to people with motor neuron disease who spend every minute of their final days/weeks/months/years in terrible pain, in fear that if they can have an easy death, their relatives will be prosecuted.

Notice how the Level 7 response includes

- Controlled use of sentence variation and structure which has been constructed intentionally to achieve the purpose.
- Sentences which are shaped and adapted to reflect the tone of the differing arguments expressed.

Next steps…

Check through your last piece of extended writing and highlight each sentence type you have used (simple/complex/compound) For each one, consider how they could be altered to relate directly to your purpose.

Chapter 4 — Shape it, sort, write it.

In what other subjects could I apply these skills?

Programme of Study Links	**Critical understanding** - assessing the validity and significance of information and ideas from different sources
Framework Objectives	**8.5** structuring, organising and presenting texts in a variety of forms on paper and on screen
	8.6 developing and using editing and proofreading skills on paper and on screen
	3.2 Taking roles in group discussion
Personal Learning & Thinking Skills	Creative thinkers
	Reflective learners
AFL	Peer and self-assessment through correction exercises and 'You're the examiner'
Assessment Focus	AF3 – organise and present whole texts effectively, sequencing and structuring information, ideas and events
	AF4 – construct paragraphs and use cohesion within and between paragraphs
Functional Skills	Writing documents on increasingly complex subjects and adapting them to suit the intended audience and purpose

Challenge 1 - Get thinking

a) Where might you see this type of text?
b) What do you think it is referring to?

inviting, original, edgy, happening, different.

When could I use these skills outside of school?

Chapter 4

In this unit I will learn how to effectively… *(Learning Objectives)*	• structure, organise and present texts in a variety of forms on paper and on screen • develop and use editing and proofreading skills on paper and on screen
The topics I will be studying are… *(Stimulus)*	How to write an effective: Leaflet/Article/Newspaper Report/Advert
My understand will be checked by seeing how I… *(Assessment Criteria)*	AF3 - organise and present whole texts effectively, sequencing and structuring information, ideas and events AF4 - construct paragraphs and use cohesion within and between paragraphs
My achievement will be demonstrated through me successfully completing the following challenges: *(Learning Outcomes)*	1) Get thinking – language exercise 2) Analysis of writing frames 3) Collective memory 4) Connecting paragraphs 5) Train reaction – image response 6) Paired connective task 7) Chain reaction bingo 8) Exploring Aims 9) Language and presentation activity 10) NSPCC paired response 11) Analysis of impact 12) Audience awareness 13) You're the examiner 14) Assess confidence levels 15) Develop editing skills 16) Adapt questions exercise 17) Parents' leaflet planning 18) Leaflet comparison 19) Exploring leaflet questions 20) Article planning 21) Question the questions 22) Exploration of how articles are shaped 23) You're the teacher 24) Quote exploration 25) Newspaper report analysis 26) Challenge the teacher 27) Newspaper report 28) Exploration of presentational devices 29) Sports/Music reporting 30) Advertising your town/village Future Skills – interview preparation

Chapter 4
Challenge 2 - Analysis of writing frames

Below are a selection of writing symbols that you may be familiar with.

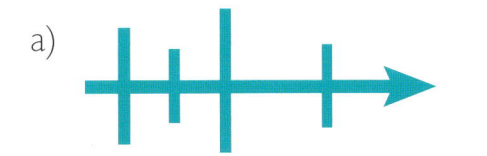

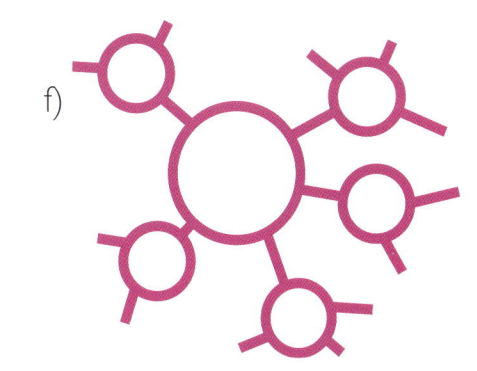

a)

b)

c)

d)

e)

f)

What has helped me learn effectively today?

a) Discuss with your learning partner what type of writing each one may symbolise. The writing types illustrated are:

- Recount/diary
- Persuade
- Explain
- Instruct
- Discuss
- Describe
- Report

b) Explain why you have made your decisions
c) Produce your own writing frame for a piece of fiction or non-writing of your choice.

101

Chapter 4 **Challenge 3**

Below is a section from a web page that you will be looking in depth later.

a) Look at this for 30 seconds and then close the text book. You then need to reproduce what you can remember about the page on a separate piece of paper.

What strategies could I use to progress further?

Uniquely Manchester

visit **manchester**

Bolton: there's a new trail in town…
Discover Bolton's inventors, presenters, crackerjacks and steeplejacks.

Cityscapes
Manchester is a dramatic mix of old and new. The futuristic design and innovative shapes of its contemporary architecture sit side by side with the spires and grinning gargoyles of its proud past

Manchester Industrial Heritage
Manchester was the trail-blazing spirit behind the Industrial Revolution of the 18th and 19th centuries, which led the world into the modern industrial era. Transport yourself back in time with the fascinating legacy of a period that changed the way we live.

b) What techniques did you use to help you remember this web page?

Structuring paragraphs effectively

How long should a paragraph be?

This depends on what you want a particular paragraph to achieve in relation to the rest of the text you are writing.

For example, if you want to draw attention to a particular event or change the tone of your writing, a very short paragraph which has followed a longer, more complex paragraph could be used.

When should I change to a new paragraph?

For a new:
- place
- time
- speaker
- viewpoint/perspective
- topic

Chapter 4

How do I construct a paragraph? What should be included?

One way of thinking about paragraphing is to visualise you going on a burger eating journey where you need to think about what should be included in the:

Top layer	Topic sentence to introduce subject of paragraph
Meat/salad in the middle	Development of your points, using description/narration/dialogue
Bottom layer	Conclusion or connection to next paragraph.

What is a topic sentence?

A topic sentence indicates to the reader the main idea that will be explored in the paragraph and is usually the first sentence.

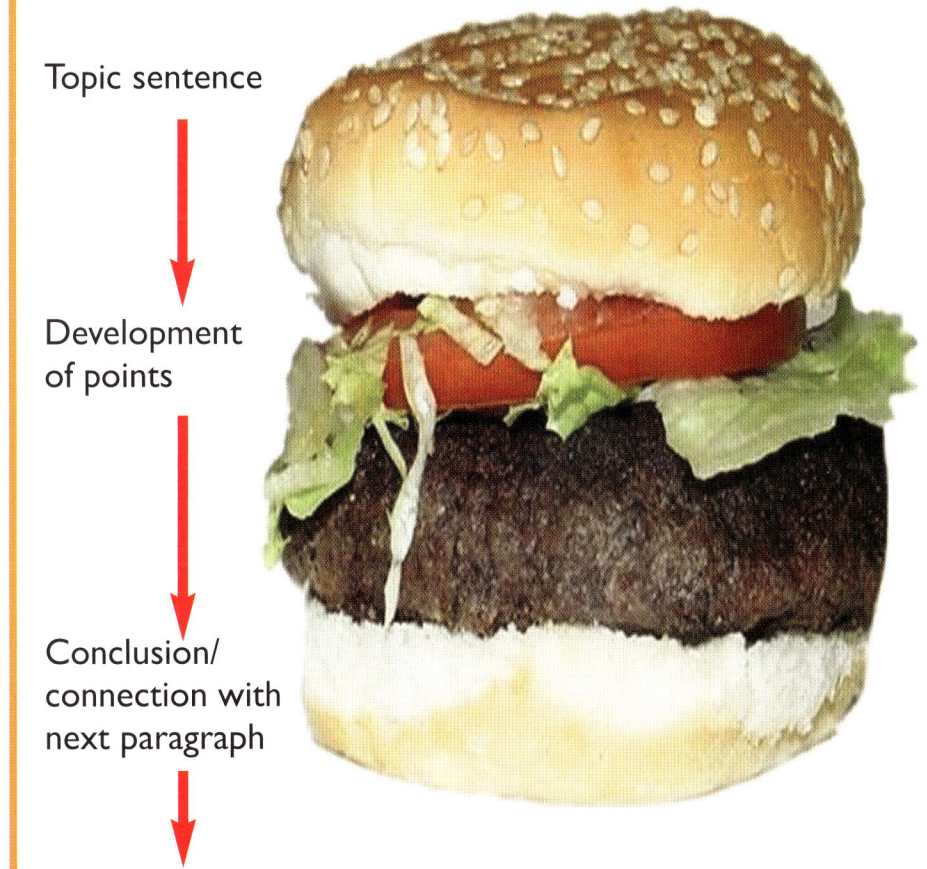

Topic sentence
↓
Development of points
↓
Conclusion/ connection with next paragraph
↓

Last summer was probably the worst I can remember.
↓
Not only did I fail my GCSEs, lose my part time job and see my pet hamster kick the bucket, I was also dumped by my girlfriend! Great stuff eh?
↓
At least September proved to be a whole new experience all together.
↓

Write the next paragraph in this sequence, using the same structure as above.

How can I connect my ideas within and between paragraphs?

Chapter 4

Challenge 4

In what other subjects could I apply these skills?

Get in the middle of a Train Reaction

Why do you think this image has been used to describe how sentences/paragraphs might be linked?

When connecting sentences and paragraphs it is important that they are linked in some way; this can be achieved through the use of:

1) Connectives (linking words which outline the relationship between two or more ideas)
2) Reference chains (where you refer to something that has been previously discussed)

Get connected - Using connectives effectively to link your ideas

You will need to connect your sentences and paragraphs in order to:	For example:
• Sequence your ideas	subsequently/ meanwhile/ at length
• Show cause and effect	consequently/ as a result / depending upon
• Include contrast and balance	however/ nevertheless/ alternatively
• Provide opinion and interpretation	one might consider/ obviously / maybe
• Make additional points	what is more / moreover / as well as
• Illustrate your points further	for example / as revealed by / in other words
• Make comparisons	equally / in juxtaposition / compared with
• Emphasise your point	above all/ specifically / in particular
• Make exceptions	only if / unless / except (for)
• Persuade your target audience	obviously/ undoubtedly / certainly
• Summarise your ideas	in a nutshell / overall / to sum up
• Conclude your written response	ultimately / in conclusion / finally

Chapter 4

Challenge 5

In chapter 1 there is a full bank of connectives that you can refer to when writing for a particular audience. In pairs, practice reading out these connectives:
a) reads out the connective
b) finishes the sentence

naturally obviously clearly evidently surely certainly decidedly

For example:
A) equally...... B) people could argue that you are better off being schooled at home.

How to link sentences by making a chain reaction

A reference chain is a simple technique that writers use when making links with previous points made. Below are some examples of how and where they can be used:

Reference chains	Examples
Actual repetition of the same word/phrase or a synonym (often for dramatic effect)	**Say no to war** to save the lives of thousands. **Say no to war** so that our children can live with hope and not fear.
Personal pronouns to refer to a character	**Suzy**, the bad tempered daughter of the local vicar, decided to leave everyone alone. **She** had caused enough trouble for one night.
Personal pronouns to entice the reader and make them speculate as to who it could be	**She** arrived outside the room, anguish etched on her face. It was **Maggie's** turn to share in the family's grief.
Abstract nouns that refer to a previous discussion	The **issue** that you mentioned regarding the boy's whereabouts is still a concern.
Determiners	The family were on their way to Lapland. **Every one** was excited.
Demonstratives	War in Gaza has cost thousands of lives. **Those** children have had to suffer for too long.
Adjectives	Robbie Keane has made a remarkable return to White Hart Lane. The **former** spurs striker today sealed a 12 million pound move.
Verbs (or verb chains)	We had already **been** to the graveyard that week…
Direct reference to a previous event/part of the text.	As outlined in the **introduction**, knife crime is still a huge problem.

When could I use these skills outside of school?

105

Chapter 4

Challenge 6

Chain reaction bingo

1) In threes, produce some new examples of reference chains
2) A) reads out the examples whilst B & C look at the bingo card and tick off when an example has been read out.

Actual repetition of the same word/phrase or a synonym (often for dramatic effect)	Personal pronouns to refer to a character	Personal pronouns to entice the reader
Abstract nouns that refer to a precious discussion	Determiners	Demonstratives
Adjectives	Verbs (or verb chains)	Direct reference to a previous event/part of the text.

Exploring writers' techniques

Writing an effective leaflet

What is a leaflet?

A leaflet is a piece of information which is presented in a booklet format which can have a variety of different purposes. They are produced in this way in order to make the material more eye-catching and easier to read.

The anti-smoking leaflet on pages 108-113 has been produced by **The British Heart Foundation (BHF)**.

Challenge 7

a) What do you think would be the aims of The British Heart Foundation?
b) Think of one image that could be used to reflect their message.

Chapter 4

Challenge 8

In pairs, read through the leaflet taking on the following roles:
a) pick the persuasive language.
b) make a list of all the presentational features that are used in the leaflet (with an example of each one) you may use a table like the one below.

Presentational Device	Where used	How does it help to get the message across?
• Graphics		
• Cartoons		
• Pictures		
• Symbols		
• Headings		
• Sub-headings		
• Diagrams		
• Use of colour		
• Logos		

In what other subjects could I apply these skills?

Chapter 4

YACK!

British Heart Foundation

An A – Z of things you always wanted to know about smoking but were too hacked to ask.

AIR & PASSIVE SMOKING

Cigarette smoke adds more than 4700 chemicals to the air for smokers and non-smokers to breath. Many are poisonous. Some are radioactive. Fifty are known to cause cancers. They include ACETIC ACID (vinegar), ACETONE (nail varnish remover), AMMONIA (cleaner), and ARSENIC (poison). And that's just some of the A's...

Hey, this party's got a great atmosphere!

>> Eyes
Source: US Surgeon General

BAN

B is for Ban, does it work?

- Does a ban on selling tobacco to under-16 year-olds work?
- Do you think there should be a total ban on smoking in public places (like in New York) in the UK?
- Will a ban on tobacco advertising lead to a decrease in tobacco consumption?
- Do you think tobacco companies sponsoring a brand of clothing (e.g. Marlboro Classics) is a form of advertising?
- Do you think Cambridge University should have accepted the £1.5m donation from a tobacco company?

✓ = YES
✗ = NO

If you were Prime Minister for a day, what legislation against smoking would you introduce?

>> Marketing

COLUMBUS

15 October 1492: Christopher Columbus lands on the island he calls San Salvador. The islanders take gifts of fruit and "certain dried leaves which give off a distinct smell". He eats the fruit but throws away the leaves because he doesn't know what to do with them.

A month later he's amazed to hear he is supposed to stick the leaves in his mouth and set fire to them. It's tobacco.

>> Gutter
Source: *Tobacco in History*, J. Goodman

108

Chapter 4

DEAD FOOT

Smoking is the biggest cause of amputations of the foot and leg. Every year in the UK, about 2000 heavy smokers lose a leg in this way. Smoke causes blood to get sticky, and blood vessels to get narrower. Blood then flows more slowly through the body.

It's worse in parts farthest away from the heart, such as the fingers and toes. When the blood supply can't reach the foot, the foot gets a disease called

>> Heart
Source: www.doh.gov.uk

EYES

You know how smoke can irritate your eyes, making them weep and turn red. Well it's the same for your pets too. Dog and cat shows, even the world famous Crufts Dog Show, have banned smoking because of the effects passive smoking has on the animals.

>> June 9th
Source: www.the-kennel-club.org.uk

FIRE

The luxury home of the boss of RJ Reynolds (one of the world's biggest cigarette companies) was recently burnt down by . . . yes, a cigarette.

>> Risk
Source: www.guardianunlimited.co.uk

GUTTER

Everyday smokers in Britain throw away 180 million butts and 12 million cigarette packs.

But cigarettes don't just *end up* in the gutter. In a sense they started life there as well.

Cigarettes were invented in the 1500s by beggars in the Spanish city of Seville. Sailors brought tobacco back to Europe as a luxury for the rich, who smoked it in pipes or rolled into cigars.

The beggars picked up cigar stubs from the street, crumbled the old tobacco into scraps of paper, then smoked them. The cigarette was born.

>> War
Source: *Tobacco in History*, J Goodman

HEART

Being smoke free greatly reduces your lifetime risk of
♥ heart disease
♥ heart attacks
♥ high blood pressure
♥ narrow arteries
♥ strokes (brain damage)
♥ blood clots
♥ chest pain
♥ irregular and fast heart beat

Smoke free blood delivers oxygen better too. So your muscles, nerves and other cells work much more efficiently.

HELP YOUR HEART – BE SMOKE FREE

>> Lights
Source: bhf.org.uk

Chapter 4

IMAGE

Some people start smoking because they think it will improve their image. In fact, the opposite happens...

Smoke stains teeth, and helps plaque to build up. Smokers are more likely to need false teeth. Gums are more likely to bleed. Skin tends to get dry and wrinkled younger in life. Smoke makes some skin conditions (such as eczema) worse. Men are more likely to lose their hair younger, and go bald. Both men and women smokers go grey earlier. Smokers often lose much of their sense of smell and taste, and more have halitosis (bad breath).

>> Kiss
Source: www.bmj.com

JUNE 9 – DON'T SMOKE IN CARS DAY

Q: Do you think people should be banned from smoking in cars if there are children on board?

In a recent survey in Australia 72% said YES. 27% said NO. 1% couldn't decide. What do YOU think?

When people smoke inside a car, passengers breathe in concentrated 'Environmental Tobacco Smoke'. (This is also called 'Passive' or 'Second-Hand' smoking.) Children and babies are more likely to suffer from asthma, runny eyes, 'glue ear', colds and many other disorders.

>> Air & Passive Smoking
Source: www.nosmoking.org.uk

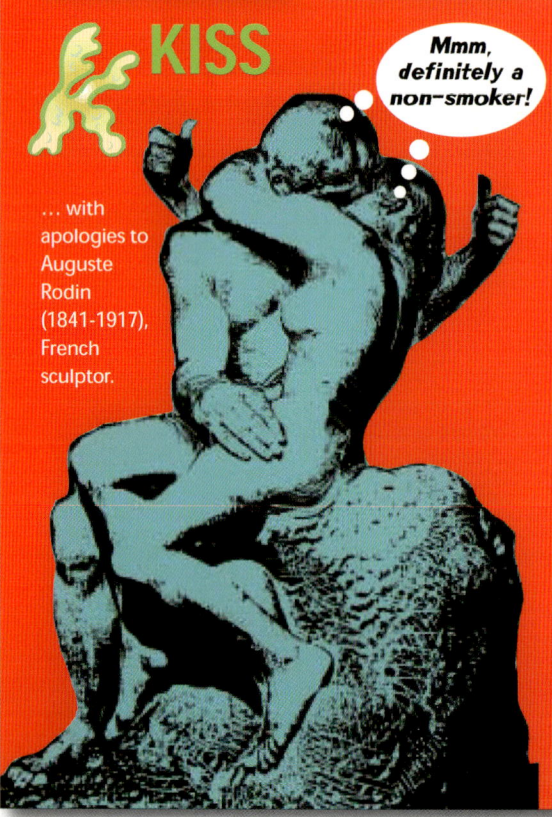

KISS

Mmm, definitely a non-smoker!

... with apologies to Auguste Rodin (1841-1917), French sculptor.

LIGHTS

'Light', 'mild' or 'low tar' cigarettes *sound* as if they're not so harmful – that's why their makers call them that.

But the smoker will probably smoke more cigarettes, and inhale more deeply, to get the same amount of nicotine (which is great for tobacco company profits).

The deeper you breathe in, the farther the tar goes down into your lungs. And you breathe even more carbon monoxide.

So the smoker's risk of a heart attack could be even greater.

>> Nicotine
Source: www.ash.org.uk

MARKETING

Companies in the UK tobacco industry have tried to hide that they work with advertising agencies to target young people. They used advertising to increase overall consumption as well as their brand share. Tobacco companies in the UK spent £25 million in one year (September 2001 – August 2002) just on visible advertising. But in November 2002 the government introduced a law banning all tobacco advertising in the UK.

>> Underage
Source: www.ash.org.uk

Chapter 4

NICOTINE

The main job of a cigarette is to give the smoker a shot of nicotine. Nicotine is the addictive drug in cigarettes that keeps people coming back for more. It also makes the heart pump faster and narrows blood vessels, pushing up blood pressure (hypertension).

>> Heart
Source: bhf.org.uk

OSTRICH

This is the name the tobacco industry calls its favourite people – their most loyal customers. These are the ones who carry on smoking themselves to death, ignoring the costs in health and money, and who don't give a thought to the non-smokers whose air they pollute.

>> Risk
Source: STAT, Massachusetts

PHLEGM

(pronounced "Flem") aka Mucus, Sputum, Oyster, Flob, Grolly, Green Gilbert.

The linings of our airways make a liquid – mucus – to catch any dust and bacteria that enter our lungs.

A carpet of tiny whip-like hairs (cilia) waft the mucus up the airways. Normally we just swallow the mucus without realising it. But smoke causes more mucus to be formed at the same time as it paralyses the cilia. So the body has to cough up the mucus instead.

A cough is our body's way of getting rid of poison chemicals in the lungs – fast. With the cilia system broken down, germs stay around to infect the linings of the lung. This means long-term smokers have to keep "clearing their chest", especially when they wake in the morning. This is to shift the "sputum" that has built up deep in their chest overnight.

Sputum is mucus mixed with pus (blood fluids, white blood cells, living and dead bacteria, and the remains of damaged cells from the linings of the lungs). It's the result of lung infection.

>> Taiwan
Source: *Cigarettes, What the Warning Label Doesn't Tell You*, ACSH

QUITTING

For friendly help and advice on how to stop smoking, ring one of these numbers:

In England QUITLINE® 0800 00 22 00 (freephone)
Asian Quitline give advice in different Asian languages 0800 00 22 44/55/66/77/88
In N Ireland SMOKERS QUITLINE 02890 66 32 81
In Scotland SMOKELINE 0800 84 84 84 (freephone)
In Cymru/Wales SMOKERS HELPLINE 0800 169 0169 (freephone)

If you're a smoker, you may not succeed first time, but the more times you try to give up, the more likely it is that you'll succeed.

About 1000 people give up for good every day.

>> eX-smokers
Source: www.quit.org.uk

Chapter 4

RISK

Take 10 young people who start smoking in their teens and carry on throughout their lives. What are they likely to die of?

- It is very unlikely indeed that any of them will be **MURDERED**
- And none will die in a **RADIATION LEAK** from a nuclear power station
- None will be killed by a **TERRORIST BOMB**
- And none will die in a **WAR**
- Almost certainly none will die in a **CAR CRASH** or from **AIDS**
- But 8 out of 10 will die before their time from diseases caused by **SMOKING CIGARETTES**.

`>> War` Source: based on estimates by Prof. Richard Peto

SMOKE FREE AIRWAYS

More and more restaurants and bars have smoke free areas, while many airlines have banned smoking altogether. Travelling in a train's smoking carriage is a very unpleasant experience – even for smokers!

`>> June 9 – Don't Smoke In Cars Day` Source: www.ash.org.uk

TAIWAN

A company in Taiwan has patented a coughing ashtray, designed to put people off smoking.

Every time a smoker flicks ash into the tray, it starts a major coughing fit.

Can YOU think of an invention that would put people off smoking?

`>> Heart` Source: www.newscientist.com

UNDERAGE SMOKERS

Why are 19% of boys and 25% of girl, regular smokers before the age of 16?

Do they think it's rebellious to be paying tax to the government at such an early age? Is it cool to be copying exactly what their parents and grandparents used to do? Is it clever to be exploited by cigarette manufacturers even before they can legally be exploited at 16?

`>> Video` Source: www.ash.org.uk

VIDEO

Whenever someone lights up a cigarette on screen, it may not be because the storyline needs it. It's more likely that the tobacco industry paid the film makers big money for it to happen.

This is a very powerful method of advertising. Named cigarette brands feature in many Hollywood films.

In fact, films get seen more on video than at the cinema, which makes them even better for tobacco companies – the videos get shown all round the world, and they get round any advertising bans or age restrictions at the cinema.

Videos get shown in the home, over and over again, often to very young children. This way the tobacco industry reaches far more people than go to the cinema.

`>> Image` Source: www.hda-online.org.uk

Chapter 4

WAR

Cigarettes love war. British soldiers first took up smoking in a big way during the Crimean War (1853-56).

They picked up the habit from Turkish gunners, who rolled tobacco in paper and used them to light the gunpowder in their cannon. Between firings, they sucked on the cigarette to keep it alight.

During the First World War (1914-18), and again in World War Two (1939-1945), troops were given a ration of cigarettes. War ended, but smoking didn't.

Now nearly twice as many Britons die every year from cigarettes than died per year in World War Two (131,000 deaths compared to about 77,000).

>> eX-smokers

Source: *Tobacco in History*, J. Goodman

eX-SMOKERS

The number of people who smoke is far smaller now than 50 years ago.

In 1948, about 2 in every 3 men smoked cigarettes. That was their peak year. For women, the peak year was 1966, when over 4 in every 10 women smoked. Since then numbers have gone down – mostly because loads of people have given up. There are now more eX-smokers than smokers.

SMOKING: A DYING HABIT
% of over-16s in Great Britain who are regular cigarette smokers

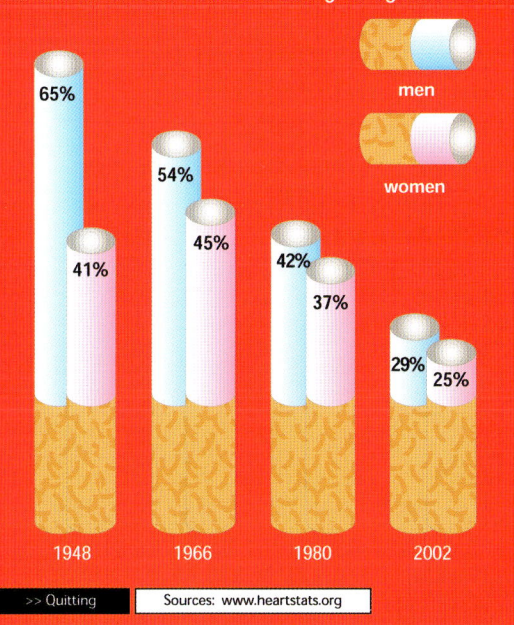

Year	Men	Women
1948	65%	41%
1966	54%	45%
1980	42%	37%
2002	29%	25%

>> Quitting   Sources: www.heartstats.org

Y-FRONTS

Male smokers are much more likely to develop impotence than non-smokers and in the UK approximately 120,000 men are impotent as a result of smoking. But a baby's problems due to smoking are only just starting. The unborn baby is more likely to abort spontaneously if the mother smokes. But then when the babies are born, more than 17,000 children under the age of five are admitted to hospital every year illness resulting from passive smoking.

>> Atmosphere   Source: University of Birmingham

ZZZZZZ

People who live with smokers are more likely to miss out on their beauty sleep – smokers are six times more likely to snore.

>> Image   Source: *Cigarettes: What The Warning Label Doesn't Tell You*, **ASCH**

Visit yheart.net and check out the smoke out section

British Heart Foundation
14 Fitzhardinge Street
London W1H 6DH

M12/2A
10/2004

© British Heart Foundation 2003. Registered Charity Number 225971

HACK! was created for the British Heart Foundation by Comic Company
www.comiccompany.co.uk Words: Philip Boys. Design: Corinne Pearlman.
Illustrations: Woodrow Phoenix, Graham Higgins. The author and artists
assert their right to be identified as creators of the work.

Chapter 4

How leaflets can be organized to create an emotional response from the reader

The following leaflet has been produced by the NSPCC (National Society for the Prevention of Cruelty to Children)

As well as the obvious presentational features that are employed to impact on the reader, the leaflet is particularly effective in developing and extending an argument through the way the sentences and paragraphs are linked.

For example

It may be easiest to do nothing. But please don't. It is important that you do something. Trust your judgement	*Sentences linked effectively through reference chains 'please don't' (do nothing) 'do something' (not nothing) 'Trust your judgement' (connects with a plea that relates to the fear of doing nothing.*

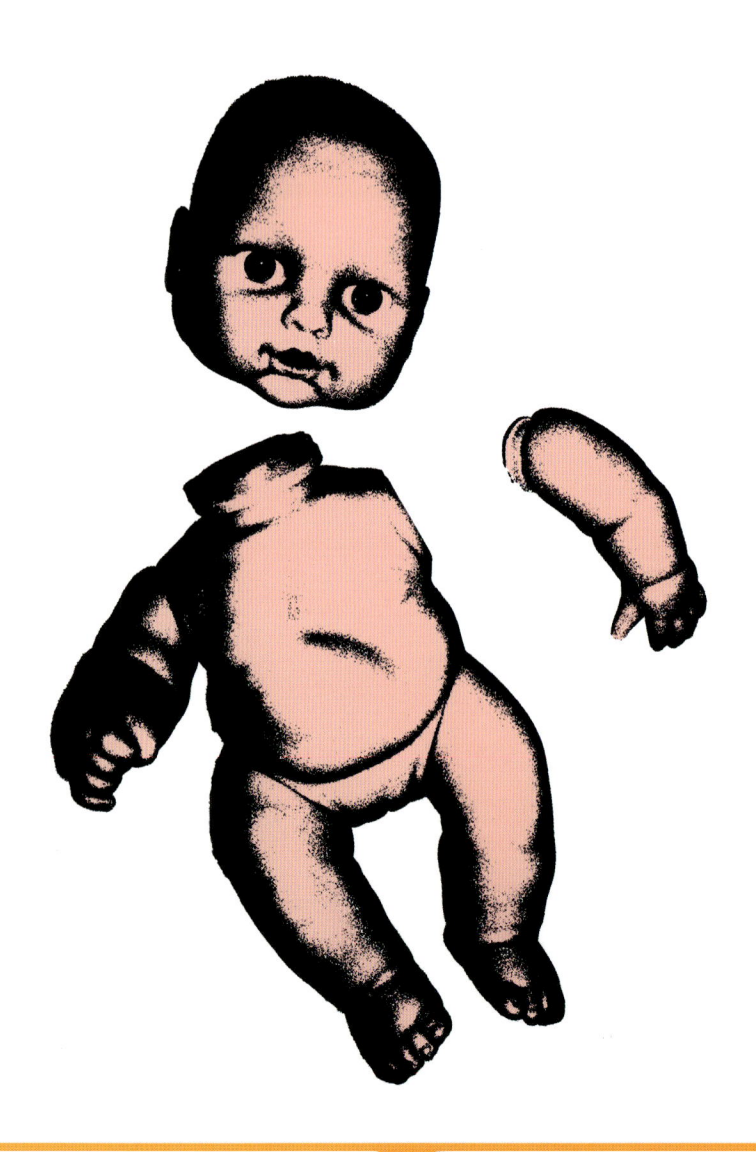

Chapter 4
Challenge 9

In threes, read through this leaflet, taking on the following roles:

a) reference chain spotter (find 5 good examples of where there are links within and between paragraphs)

b) presentation prober (find 5 good presentational features and explain why you think this)

Are you worried about the safety of a child?

Do you know a child that's always bruised?

Do you know a child that's neglected and withdrawn?

Do you hear a baby crying constantly?

Do you know a stressed parent who cannot cope?

Every action counts.
If you have concerns there is someone who will listen.
Don't keep it to yourself.
Do something

NSPCC
Cruelty to children must stop. FULL STOP.

Chapter 4

Child protection isn't just for the professionals

There's something you can do...

If you have concerns

It can be difficult to know what to do for the best. There may be good reasons for how the child seems. Maybe you don't want to antagonise your neighbours or make matters worse for the child. Perhaps you're worried the family might be broken up and the children put in care (though this rarely happens). You may think the problem will resolve itself on its own. You may not know where to go for help.

It may seem easiest to do nothing. But please don't. It is important you do something. Trust your judgement.

Every action counts

Together we can stop cruelty to children. All of us must be ready to act. This leaflet provides advice on what to do, however it can't cover every aspect of child abuse. If you still have concerns you can always telephone or email the NSPCC Child Protection Helpline, for free 24-hour advice.

Do you know a child that is constantly 'put down', insulted, sworn at or humiliated?

Why we all need to help protect children

It's estimated that at least one child is killed each week by their parents or carers. Thousands more suffer serious harm at the hands of those who are supposed to be caring for them. We know that in two thirds of cases the child abuse goes unreported at the time and many children are forced to suffer in silence.

Chapter 4

What can you do?

You can help transform the protection of children in this country and cut the amount of abuse suffered by children. Here's where to start:

All adults can ...

- Try to understand the seriousness and consequences of child abuse. Recognise the signs of abuse.
- Be someone to turn to for a child, vulnerable parent or carer. Support families in difficulty. Be there to listen.
- Trust your judgement when in doubt.
- If you have serious concerns about a child, contact social services, the police, or the free 24-hour NSPCC Child Protection Helpline.
- If you are worried and don't know what to do, contact the free 24-hour NSPCC Child Protection Helpline for advice – you can call anonymously.

Parents can ...

- Try to understand the seriousness and consequences of child abuse. Learn about healthy child development, and how to build strong families.
- Listen to children – try to understand what they're saying and doing, and why.
- Know what goes on in your children's school and how it responds to issues of child abuse and bullying.
- Find someone to turn to if you're under stress. All parents become stressed from time to time.
- Don't cross the line and hurt your children. Take alternative actions – for example, "count to ten and think again".
- If you find being a parent tough to handle, contact Parentline Plus. If you live in Northern Ireland, call the Parents Advice Centre.
- Seek child protection help and advice. If you're concerned about your children's safety – contact the NSPCC Child Protection Helpline, social services or the police.

Children and young people can ...

- Learn how to keep yourself safe. Ask your parents and teachers for advice on safety measures.
- Support your friends if they tell you they're being abused – encourage them to tell a trusted adult.
- Remember, being abused is never your choice and never your fault. Child abuse is never right.
- Find someone to turn to if you're being abused. Tell an adult you trust – maybe a teacher. Keep telling them until someone listens and takes action.
- Phone Childline or the NSPCC Child Protection Helpline if you're being abused, or know someone who is.

Do you know a child that is left alone, dirty, hungry or inadequately dressed?

Chapter 4

How can I use these techniques in my own writing?

One of the key elements of writing an effective leaflet, is that you communicate your message in a clear and concise way; this means that your choice of words, and the way you organise your content is vitally important – the layout features should complement your writing - not stand alone. In other words, don't get too fussed about having a wonderful array of font sizes, graphics and colours (that's the easy bit) as it is more important to use the appropriate facts and opinions, depending on your purpose and intended audience.

Challenge 10

a) With a learning partner, briefly rate the leaflet in terms of its impact on you as a reader:

1 – really effective – 5 no effect on me whatsoever

b) Explain why you have made this decision. What was it about this leaflet that had an impact on you?

c) What would you have changed about this leaflet to have a greater impact on you?

Challenge 11

Audience awareness

You can classify an audience into categories such as:
Age/gender/occupation/class/interest groups.

The people who produce leaflets for organizations like NSPCC follow the same procedure as advertising companies; namely they need to identify with the needs of their target audience and adapt their product/message accordingly.

The success of any persuasive text can be judged on the impact it has on its audience.

How might the following audiences respond to this leaflet?

- Child
- Parent
- Teacher

It is important that you are able to put yourself in the shoes (and mind!) of the target audience and respond accordingly.

Chapter 4

Three pupils were asked to complete the following task:

How does the leaflet by the NSPCC persuade its audience to be more aware of cruelty to children?

For each pupil make a positive comment on their response and make a suggestion on how they could improve

Pupil A

The NSPCC persuades people by telling them about all the problems that children deal with and they try to get you to stop it.

Pupil B

The leaflet uses both rhetorical devices and emotive language to good effect. The phrase "Do you know a child that's always bruised?" helps to startle the reader into taking notice of vulnerable children.

Pupil C

The article uses words such as "Are you worried about the safety of a child?" and "Do you know a child that's always bruised?" to make the reader feel sympathy for children who are at risk of neglect or abuse.

Chapter 4

Read through the following 3 questions. Rate how confident you now feel in answering them. Explain why you feel most confident to your learning partner.
1. Pick out the 5 most effective rhetorical questions. Explain why you have chosen these.
2. Persuasive language is evident throughout this leaflet. Comment on some of the writer's use of emotive language. How does it make the reader feel?
3. Comment on the layout of the leaflet. How might this appeal to the target audience?

Developing and using editing and proof reading skills

You have probably been asked numerous times to do some (if not all) one of the following to a piece of writing that you(or someone else) has produced:

- Proofread
- Edit
- Revise
- Rewrite
- Redraft

In the following section there will be some advice on how to develop these skills in order to improve your final written outcome. It is important that you don't interpret any of the above list as 'rewrite in your best handwriting' as the presentation of your work is only one aspect you need to focus on when looking for potential improvements.

Proof reading involves checking for errors in spelling/punctuation/grammar whereas **editing** involves picking out key features of a text in order to adapt the piece of text into a different style/audience. Once this process is complete, the **redrafting/revising** section involves taking on these changes to make overall improvements to your writing.

Proof reading
Checking for technical errors using skimming and scanning

a) **Skimming** – getting a sense of what the whole text is about through glancing over the whole piece of information.

b) **Scanning** – finding a particular piece of information for analysis

  1) In pairs, skim over the piece of text on the next page and pick out any errors in spelling, punctuation and grammar.

  2) Re-read the last piece of written work you have produced and proof read, using the same technique.

Chapter 4

> he stepped into the room and sit down heavily in a white plastic chair. Alan Johnston, he said in English. "We know everything." He sed that my kidnapping was about securing the release of muslims jailed in britain. Crucially, he said that I would eventually be allowed to leave. I asked when but he just said When the time is right.

Challenge 12 – developing editing skills

On the next few pages is a crime prevention booklet that was put together by the government. For this challenge you need to rewrite the booklet onto a side of A5 (half A4) for a teenage audience.

a) With your learning partner, consider:
   1) What you will need to select
   2) What must you leave out?
   3) What must you add?

b) Swap your responses with another pairing and rate each other's response by asking the following question:

How likely are you to take notice of this leaflet?
1 extremely likely – 5 not likely at all

When could I use these skills outside of school?

Chapter 4

YOUR PRACTICAL GUIDE TO CRIME PREVENTION

Home Office

Personal safety

The chances that you or a member of your family will be a victim of violent crime is low. Violent crimes are still comparatively rare and account for a very small part of recorded crime. Nevertheless, many people are frightened that they, or someone close to them, will be the victim of a violent attack.

The best way to minimise the risk of attack is by taking sensible precautions. Most people already do this as part of their everyday lives, often without realising it. You may already be aware of some of the suggestions listed below, but some may be new to you, and you may find them useful. They may seem particularly relevant to women, but if you are a man, don't stop reading or turn the page. You can act positively to contribute towards women's safety, as well as reducing the risk of assault on yourself.

How can you stay safe?
At home

• Make sure your house or flat is secure. Always secure outside doors. If you have to use a key, keep it nearby - you may need to get out quickly in the event of fire.
• If other people such as previous tenants could still have keys that fit, change the locks. Don't give keys to workmen or tradesmen, as they can easily make copies.
• If you wake to hear the sound of an intruder, only you can decide how best to handle the situation. You may want to lie quietly to avoid attracting attention to yourself, in the hope that they will leave. Or you may feel more confident if you switch on the lights and make a lot of noise by moving about. Even if you're on your own, call out loudly to an imaginary companion – most burglars will flee empty-handed rather than risk a confrontation. Ring the police as soon as it's safe for you to do so. A telephone extension in your bedroom will make you feel more secure as it allows you to call the police immediately, without alerting the intruder.
• Draw your curtains after dark and if you think there is a prowler outside – dial 999.

Never reveal any information about yourself to a stranger, and never say you are alone.

Chapter 4

YOUR PRACTICAL GUIDE TO CRIME PREVENTION — Home Office

Personal safety

- Use only your surname and initials in the telephone directory, on the doorplate, and, if you have one, beside an entry system button. That way a stranger won't know whether a man or a woman lives there.
- If you see signs of a break-in at your home, like a smashed window or open door, don't go in. The burglar may be inside. Go to a neighbour and call the police.
- If you are selling your home, don't show people around on your own. Ask your estate agent to send a representative with anyone who wants to view your house. Only employ professional accredited estate agents, removers and other trades people. Take care who you pass your keys to.
- You should of course be extremely careful about letting people into your home if you do not know them particularly well. If you do, but start to feel uneasy or threatened, don't hesitate to leave yourself. Make an excuse, such as "I think I heard the cat at the door", and go to a neighbour or a friend and ask them to come back with you, or call the police.
- When you answer the phone, simply say "hello"; don't give your number. If the caller claims to have a wrong number, ask him or her to repeat the number required. Never reveal any information about yourself to a stranger and never say you are alone in the house.
- If you receive an abusive or threatening phone call, put the receiver down beside the phone, and walk away. Come back a few minutes later and replace the receiver; don't listen to hear if the caller is still there. Don't say anything – an emotional reaction is just what the caller wants. This allows the caller to say what he or she wants to say, without causing distress to you. If the calls continue, tell the police and the operator and keep a record of the date, time and content of each phone call. This may help the authorities trace the caller.

Try not to walk too closely behind a woman out late at night or on her own.

123

Chapter 4

Challenge 13

Revising and redrafting to make improvements

Read through the following questions which refer to the original personal safety booklet. **Rewrite** these questions based on your new leaflet.

1. What use is made of the pictures and captions? How does it increase the booklet's effectiveness?
2. Comment on the headlines/subheadings and use of bullet points. Why have these been used? Comment on whether they help to get the booklet's message across.
3. Analyse the tone of the first section (before How can you stay safe?) How are the aims of booklet presented in this section? Pick out key words and phrases which may reassure the reader.
4. Do you take any crime prevention measures? Comment on which ones you don't take. For example do you 'Walk facing the traffic so a car cannot pull up beside you unnoticed' Pick out any measures you don't take and explain why you don't feel the need to take them.
5. Is the leaflet successful in raising awareness of crime prevention? Has it convinced you that you should take a more active part in your Personal Safety? Do you feel more or less safe as a result of reading the booklet? What could have been improved in the booklet? (Provide detailed examples)

Challenge 14

You have been asked to produce an information leaflet for parents, in which you advise them on how they could be better parents and have a better relationship with their teenage children.

In a small group, you need to plan what you would need to include; in particular consider the

- content (fact and opinions)
- layout – headings/sub-headings
- language used
- length

Challenge 15

Once you have completed the planning, compare your ideas with the following leaflet from Parentline Plus. Before completing your leaflet, you now need to consider:

1) What was effective about Parentline Plus' leaflet?
2) What could have been improved?
3) What changes you would make to your own ideas? (if any)

Chapter 4

GOT A TEENAGER?

Part of the TEENS' series

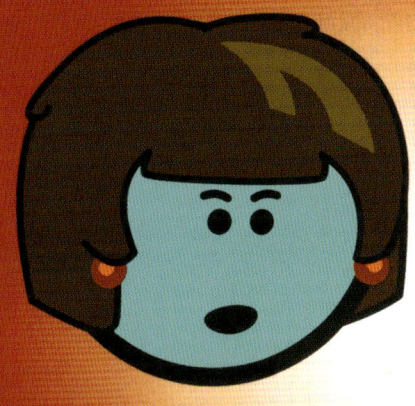

I try to tell her enough's enough.

It's easy to think your teenager doesn't want anything more to do with you. When they seem to ignore all you say or do, it's difficult to see that being a teenager can be very tough.

Free Parentline
0808 800 2222

Free Textphone
0800 783 6783

Website
www.parentlineplus.org.uk

Email
parentsupport@parentlineplus.org.uk

Parentlineplus
because instructions aren't included
0808 800 2222
www.parentlineplus.org.uk

Chapter 4

WHAT YOU CAN DO

Sometimes the things that your teenager says may hurt you. They seem to have changed from the cooperative child you once knew. But remember they are growing up to be young adults. They need to learn how to think and act for themselves but most of all they need your love, help and advice to make sense of it all.

Parentline Plus tips

- Keep an open mind and listen to their point of view.

- Change the way you talk to them. Rather than nagging, just chat when you get the opportunity such as before they go to their room, or after watching TV.

- Agree boundaries with all those involved in bringing up your children. Knowing there are rules helps your teenagers feel safe and secure.

- Understand why they may be behaving badly. They may be moody or have 'attitude' because they find it hard to put their worries into words.

- Compromise. Sometimes it is worth meeting them half way. It shows you have listened to them.

- Start to give them some responsibility for their own safety but make sure you have discussed the best ways to keep safe first.

- Enjoy your teenager as a young adult and let them know when you are proud of them.

Chapter 4

SETTING LIMITS

Boundaries are about setting the bottom line. They show what you value, and what's right for you and your family. They are the principles that guide you and help you to keep your child safe and secure. Teenagers will often test the limits you have set them – it's part of growing up.

Parentline Plus tips

- Tell your children clearly what you want and why, and listen to their point of view. Boundaries work far better if they are made and agreed by everyone.

- Make a compromise. It doesn't mean you're giving in but shows that you value their opinions and are letting your children take more responsibility for themselves.

- Trust them. Children are far more likely to cooperate if they feel trusted and part of a team.

- Give your teenagers some responsibility for their own safety as they get older. Give them ideas about how they can keep themselves safe.

- If it's not working talk over why not and make a new rule or agreement together. Be prepared to talk about or change the boundaries right through the teenage years as your children grow and mature.

→ NEW WEBSITE
www.gotateenager.org.uk

Parentline Plus has just launched a brand new social networking website for parents of teenagers. Whether you are worried about drugs and unsafe sex or just can't seem to get through the day without a row, then you are not alone. Meet other parents online and share the challenges and successes of parenting your child through the teenage years. Features include message boards, e-learning modules, interactive TV shows for parents and much more…

Chapter 4

Look through the following leaflet tasks. For each one decide on the following:
a) What information would I need to complete this task effectively
b) How confident you feel in achieving a good outcome? (1-5)

Writing to...	Theme	Task
• Persuade	Smoking	Produce at leaflet for parents where you advise them of the dangers of smoking and the physical and emotional effect it could have on their children
• Argue	Euthanasia	Produce an information leaflet from the Pro Life movement in which you argue that people should be given a choice on whether they live or die.
• Advise	Crime	Using the information from the Home Office produce an advice leaflet for teachers on how the police could be used effectively in schools.
• Inform	Pressures of Young People	Write an information leaflet aimed at teachers in which you persuade them to be more sympathetic to the problems that teenagers have.
• Discuss	Homelessness	Produce a leaflet from a student council where you discuss the issue of how best to help the homeless.

Before beginning any leaflet, remember you need to:

- achieve your purpose;
- be aware of your target audience;
- vary your tone and vocabulary to suit the needs of your purpose and audience;
- structure your leaflet in an informative and appealing way.

Chapter 4

Using sources effectively

When producing an effective article it is important to have a mixture of facts and opinions which would include personal responses from those people (who may be an individual or someone who is representing a company) who have an interest in the topic.

Read through the next article and consider how sources are used effectively to structure the information.

Jeremy Laurance
Health Editor

It was the first unmistakable warning from an official body about the dangers of tobacco. *Smoking and health*, published 40 years ago this week, is still regarded as the most significant report the Royal College of Physicians has produced. Yet four decades later, smoking is still by far the greatest threat to public health.

They are 40 years in which five million people in the UK have died from smoking, 12 times as many as were killed in the Second World War. Forty years in which successive governments have responded to the call for curbs on smoking with procrastination, special pleading and half measures. Forty years in which cigarettes have been proved beyond doubt to kill yet are still promoted, glamorised and marketed to the young.

To mark this sombre anniversary, the Royal College of Physicians published a new report yesterday, *Forty fatal years*, jointly with Ash, the anti-smoking campaign group, charting the missed opportunities and government failures that have sent so many smokers to an early death. Launching the report, Professor Sir George Alberti, president of the college, said: "It is shameful that 40 years on we still have so many unnecessary preventable deaths from smoking. We must have widespread urgent action now."

Clive Bates, director of Ash, said great hopes had greeted the Labour government's manifesto pledge in 1997 to tackle smoking but progress since had been disappointing.

The latest attempt to ban tobacco advertising, in a Private Member's Bill currently before the House of Lords, is dependent for its success on government support, which is still in the balance. Mr Bates said: "If this Bill is not given parliamentary time it will reveal something dark about this Government. I sense a nervousness about tobacco in Number 10."

Government equivocation over the dangers of smoking was clear from the start. After Sir Richard Doll published his ground-breaking study in 1950 which was the first to make the link between tobacco and lung cancer, the public and political response was sceptical. Smoking was endemic and respectable and the tobacco industry was a major contributor to the Exchequer. When Ian Macleod, the health minister, finally agreed to hold a press conference on the findings four years later in February 1954 – he chain smoked throughout the meeting.

Three years later in 1957 the government released a statement on smoking that established its policy for the remainder of the century. It denied it had a duty to warn the public and insisted that smoking was a matter for individual choice.

Publication of the Royal College of Physicians' report in 1962 marked a watershed. Written for the ordinary reader it gained wide press coverage. From that point the tide began to turn against smoking.

Smoking was still ubiquitous in the early Sixties, with 70 per cent of men and 43 per cent of women regular smokers. Today, the figures are down to 29 per cent of men and 25 per cent of women. So although five million have died, it is possible to claim that between 1.5 and 1.8 million lives have been saved.

Chapter 4

One of the greatest restraints on government action was the perceived reliance of the Treasury on cigarette taxes, which accounted for 14 per cent of public revenue in 1962. Today that has fallen to 3 per cent yet the myth that the Government is constrained from acting against tobacco by economic considerations persists.

The tobacco companies mounted a fierce campaign to defend their market. When direct advertising was restricted, the industry moved into sports sponsorship, including Formula One motor racing, and an estimated £130m a year is now spent on promotion backed by a carefully orchestrated disinformation campaign about the risks of smoking.

Sir Richard Doll, who attended yesterday's press conference, said it would be a mistake to put the main effort into preventing the young from taking up smoking, because it was likely to have the opposite effect and encourage them to smoke. That was why the tobacco industry had promoted the strategy. "I learnt that 50 years ago," he said.

Sir Richard, who smoked 20 a day until his own research convinced him of the dangers of the habit, said it was never too late to give up. He said: "At 30 the risk is almost totally eliminated and at 50 to 60 you can live a more enjoyable life as well as a longer one. My message is, stop smoking, enjoy life more and enjoy more of it."

Seven steps to fighting the rise in tobacco consumption

The Royal College of Physicians' report contained seven recommendations "to curb the present rising consumption of tobacco".

1 **More public education on the hazards of smoking**.
Anti-tobacco spending was derisory until 1998 when £50m was introduced for a three-year campaign. That has been criticised by Ash for dissipating sums on too many small initiatives, providing weak or incoherent messages and leaving £8m unspent.

2 **More restrictions on the sale of tobacco to children.**
Selling cigarettes to under-16s has been an offence for many years but enforcement is patchy. The value of cigarettes sold to teenagers is 2,000 times the level of fines imposed on retailers.

3 **Restriction of tobacco advertising.**
Television advertising of tobacco was banned in the mid-Sixties but the tobacco companies responded by investing in televised sport. A near-complete ban on tobacco advertising was a manifesto commitment of the Labour government in 1997 and 2001 – but hopes are now pinned on a Private Member's Bill currently before the House of Lords.

4 **Restriction on smoking in public places.**
Progress has been made in the private sector. But the Government has failed to make a smoke-free workplace a right.

5 **Increased tax on cigarettes.**
Taxation has increased substantially but smokers have responded by trading down, switching to hand-rolling tobacco and the black market. Actual prices have not increased very much.

6 **Information on tar and nicotine content.**
The difficulty is providing information that is meaningful. Smokers compensate for less tar and nicotine by taking deeper puffs or more puffs.

7 **Anti-smoking clinics.**
Not until 1999 was smoking cessation regarded as a mainstream NHS treatment – and there is still a long way to go. Nicotine therapy is now available on prescription and £20m a year is being invested in smoking cessation clinics.

Chapter 4

Challenge 20

The writer of this article uses a variety of sources to support their article:

Source:	a) Explain why you think each source was used by Jeremy Laurance
Professor Sir George Alberti	
Clive Bates	
Sir Richard Doll	
Ian Macleod	
In 1957 the government released a statement	
Publication of the Royal College of Physicians' report	
The tobacco companies	

Future Skills

If you were writing an article on the how the smoking ban has affected your local community
a) Who might you want to speak to?
b) What questions would you ask them?
c) What would be your own personal view?

When could I use these skills outside of school?

Chapter 4 — Challenge 21

In what other subjects could I apply these skills?

a) If you were asked to answer one of the following questions, which one would help you become a better writer of a newspaper report?

1. Why do you think the writer discusses the history of smoking in this article?
2. Pick out 5 facts from the article which best represents the argument on the dangers of smoking to health.
3. Comment on how the actions of Ian Macleod might have had a negative impact on raising awareness of the dangers of smoking.
4. What are your views on tobacco advertising? Should it be allowed for certain events? Does it make any difference to whether people smoke or not? Give reasons for your answer.
5. Go through each of the 7 points made at the end on the article. Give a personal response to each one.

b) What other question would help you become a better writer of articles?

Articles that explore a controversial issue

As well as informing the public of a recent news event, an article can also be used to spark a debate on an emotive issue; it is interesting to see how some writers will obviously bring their on viewpoints on a topic even though they are expected to give an impartial view.

In this article, Kathy Marks presents a case which examines the issue of Euthanasia, a term used to describe voluntary death – illegal in the UK and Australia, where the story was reported. In some countries, such as Holland, Euthanasia is legal. This is a story about a woman who committed suicide in front of 21 of her family and friends who now may face imprisonment. As you read the article, consider how the report may influence your opinion on such a controversial issue.

Chapter 4

Family faces jail for watching cancer victim kill herself

By Kathy Marks in Sydney
24 May 2002

After three years of enduring the agony of bowel cancer, Nancy Crick decided enough was enough. She swallowed an overdose of drugs, took a swig of Baileys and lit a final cigarette.

Yesterday, her home on the Gold Coast in Queensland, Australia, was declared a crime scene and 21 friends and relatives who watched her commit suicide faced the possibility of life imprisonment.

Mrs Crick, a 69-year-old former barmaid, had made no secret of her desire to end her life, chronicling her physical deterioration in graphic detail in an internet diary. She did not want to die alone, but she knew that assisting a suicide was illegal, so on the eve of her death she recorded a video statement aimed at protecting her loved ones.

"It's my death, I'm doing it and no one else," she declared in the video. Mrs Crick, who campaigned vociferously for the reform of euthanasia laws, said: "I can't take any more pain and suffering. I just can't."

Her life had become an endless round of pain, medication, vomiting and diarrhoea, she explained. "I can't even hold my great-grandson. I can't do a darned thing."

Australia's Northern Territory became the first place in the world to legalise voluntary euthanasia in 1996, but the law was overturned by the federal government nine months later, after four terminally ill patients had taken their lives. The Netherlands legalised euthanasia last month, and Belgium is preparing to follow suit.

In Australia, people merely present during a suicide can be prosecuted for assisting. Forensic police in blue overalls sealed off Mrs Crick's home in the small town of Burleigh Heads early yesterday, shortly after her body was carried out to a waiting ambulance.

Officers will decide whether to bring charges after questioning everyone who was with her on Wednesday night, including a witness aged 94. It was at 8.30pm that evening that Mrs Crick carried out a promise she had made two months previously to kill herself before the onset of winter. She had obtained the relevant drugs after an appeal on the internet. Dr Philip Nitschke, Australia's foremost euthanasia advocate and an adviser to Mrs Crick, said her death was dignified and peaceful.

Dr Nitschke, who assisted the four deaths in the Northern Territory, said: "She drank her drugs and decided to have a glass of Baileys to follow. She only had a sip of the Baileys. She said 'I feel like a cigarette' and while she was lighting up that cigarette, she slipped into unconsciousness and died 20 minutes later."

Her death has reignited the euthanasia debate and presented the authorities with a quandary. How can they prosecute people for helping to bring about a death that was so ardently desired? Yet how can they ignore such a flagrant flouting of the law? Terry O'Gorman, a lawyer for the witnesses, said that to bring a prosecution would be "a total travesty".

The state premier, Peter Beattie, offered his condolences to Mrs Crick's family but reiterated his opposition to changing the law. "I've given a lot of thought to it and I want to protect people. I want to protect life," he said.

Dr Nitschke had urged Mrs Crick to take up an offer of palliative care at Gold Coast Hospital in April, but she left after a few days, saying it had not helped her significantly. As well as recording the video before she died, she gave two television interviews, which were broadcast last night. Asked in one whether she was afraid of dying, she replied: "I'm afraid of living, of what's going to happen every day I get up, what pain I'm going through." In the video, she said: "The thing that upsets me most is that the law says I can kill myself any time I want to, but no one can be with me because they might have helped me. That's just rubbish and I don't see why I should die alone. I don't want to die alone."

Chapter 4 **Challenge 22**

Exploring the way that the writer shapes the story

The writer appears to sympathise with the tragic story of Nancy Crink, as well as the supporting the case for legalising Euthanasia. Make notes on how Kathy Marks attempts to present the case for legalising Euthanasia. The first couple have been done for.

Family faces jail for watching cancer victim kill herself

By Kathy Marks in Sydney
24 May 2002

After three years of enduring the agony of bowel cancer, Nancy Crick decided enough was enough. She swallowed an overdose of drugs, took a swig of Baileys and lit a final cigarette.

Yesterday, her home on the Gold Coast in Queensland, Australia, was declared a crime scene and 21 friends and relatives who watched her commit suicide faced the possibility of life imprisonment.

Mrs Crick, a 69-year-old former barmaid, had made no secret of her desire to end her life, chronicling her physical deterioration in graphic detail in an internet diary. She did not want to die alone, but she knew that assisting a suicide was illegal, so on the eve of her death she recorded a video statement aimed at protecting her loved ones.

"It's my death, I'm doing it and no one else," she declared in the video. Mrs Crick, who campaigned vociferously for the reform of euthanasia laws, said: "I can't take any more pain and suffering. I just can't."

Her life had become an endless round of pain, medication, vomiting and diarrhoea, she explained. "I can't even hold my great-grandson. I can't do a darned thing."

Juxtaposition of two conflicting paragraphs helps to create a dramatic effect, further increasing the reader's sympathy for the victim and outrage of the police's involvement

Matter of fact tone increases the impact

Use of emotive language to focus the reader's attention on the suffering.

Chapter 4

Challenge 23

You're the teacher

The student below was asked to comment on how effectively the article influences the reader's view of Euthanasia. You need to say something positive and set a target for improvement.

> The article tries to make you believe that you should be able to kill yourself as long as your family are there. It is a story about a woman who had cancer and wanted to die but her family are getting in trouble cos the police said they watched her die.

Challenge 24

Below are a selection of quotations from the article you have been exploring. With your learning partner, rank each quote 1 – 10 in terms of which quote is most effective in supporting the view that Euthanasia should be legalised?

1 – most effective – 10 least effective

1) Mrs Crick, a 69-year-old former barmaid had made no secret of her desire to end her life, chronicling her physical deterioration in graphic detail

2) On the eve of her death she recorded a video statement aimed at protecting her loved ones.

3) "It's my death, I'm doing it and no one else."

4) Her life had become an endless round of pain, medication, vomiting and diarrhoea.

5) Officers will decide whether to bring charges after questioning everyone who was with her on Wednesday night, including a witness aged 94.

6) Dr Philip Nitschke, Australia's foremost euthanasia advocate and an adviser to Mrs Crick, said her death was dignified and peaceful.

7) How can they prosecute people for helping to bring about a death that was so ardently desired?

8) Terry O'Gorman, a lawyer for the witnesses, said that to bring a prosecution would be "a total travesty".

9) "I'm afraid of living, of what's going to happen every day I get up, what pain I'm going through."

10) "I don't see why I should die alone. I don't want to die alone."

What strategies could I use to progress further?

When could I use these skills outside of school?

Chapter 4

Using reported and direct speech effectively in newspaper articles.

Direct speech:

"They were a very small part of the story," said Mr. Holcroft

Reported speech:

She and her husband Mick, Ms Whitear's stepfather, added that they had been taken aback by the media frenzy surrounding the photographs.

Read through the article below and consider how the writer presents the emotional story of Rachel Whitear.

The Guardian - 02 March 2002

Experts divided on whether shock tactics will deter young people.

By Sarah Hall

The parents of a 21-year-old university dropout who died of a heroin overdose last night justified their decision to release graphic photographs of her blackened corpse as part of an educational video.

Pauline Holcroft, the mother of Rachel Whitear, a one-time psychology and sociology student, who was pictured still clutching the syringe used for her fatal fix, said: "We realised when we agreed to release them they would be distasteful to some people but we felt they were a very important part of the film."

She and her husband Mick, Ms Whitear's stepfather, added that they had been taken aback by the media frenzy surrounding the photographs, and that they should be seen in the context of the 22-minute film, which charts the effect her descent into addiction had on her middle-class family.

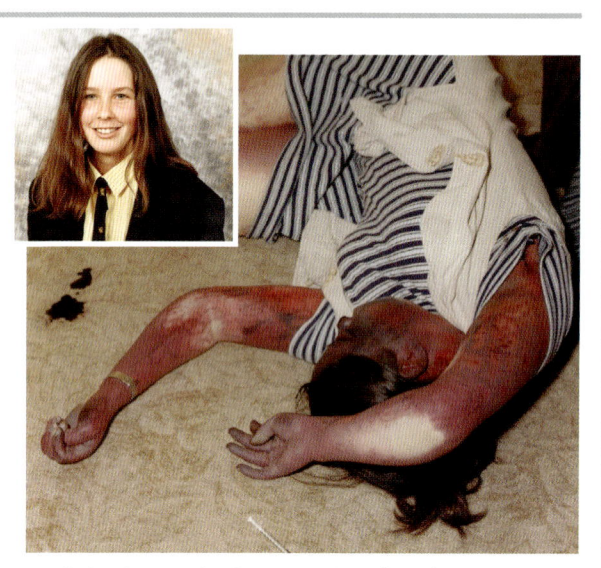

Rachel Whitear, the former student (inset) whose death photographs (main) were released by her parents.

"They were a very small part of the story," said Mr Holcroft, of Ledbury, Herefordshire. "People need to see the whole video. To us these photographs are not that shocking."

Mrs Holcroft added: "I think we are focusing too much on one small part. The exposure of these photographs is an important part of the film, but it's only one part and others are equally important." Poems written by Ms Whitear as she fought unsuccessfully to overcome her addiction were more emotive.

Chapter 4

"The feedback we have got from parents is excellent. Practically 100% of children said it would make them think they couldn't do this to their families," Mrs Holcroft said.

As the graphic images were displayed on news stands yesterday, opinion was divided on whether such shock tactics would work, with some drugs specialists warning that such images would have little effect on drugs deaths, which have almost doubled from 864 in 1993 to 1,662 in 2000.

But Paul Betts, who first employed the tactic by releasing a picture of his daughter Leah, lying in intensive care after taking ecstasy, said there was no question that such stark images shocked young people from their complacent belief that they were impervious to the fatal effect of drugs.

"Our release of the picture of Leah and the video we made afterwards has been hailed by young people as the best drugs awareness information package they have seen," he said yesterday. "I've been to over 3,200 schools, spoken to 2.3m young people and 500,000 parents and I've had over half a million letters from young people who say that, after having heard me, they're packing up taking drugs.

"While shock tactics won't work for everybody they will work for some and what we must never forget is that if you just save one person's life, it's been worthwhile."

The former Met police officer added that he did not regret "for a moment" releasing Leah's picture after she collapsed after taking the drug on her 18th birthday in 1995.

There was agreement from Rosie Brocklehurst, of Addiction, the national drug treatment charity, who insisted: "These pictures do have an effect, because they make people sit up and listen."

Lynn Clare, project manager of the support group Parents Against Drug Abuse, said: "It has certainly caused a lot of interest here: our phones have been inundated since early morning. A lot of the time parents will know something's wrong and not be sure, and this sort of publicity prompts them to seek help."

Yet she admitted the images themselves - as opposed to the video - would probably have little effect on their target market: secondary school pupils.

"It probably won't have any more of an effect on children because they don't equate themselves with this and they tend to think they are fairly indestructible. When the Leah Betts picture was shown, it caused a lot of interest but it didn't stop people taking ecstasy," she said.

Herefordshire local education authority - which has produced the video which charts Ms Whitear's descent to a lonely death in a flat in Exmouth, Devon - says that students who had seen it had been affected because it "challenges the stereotypical image of a drug user".

But the drugs charity, DrugScope, yesterday insisted that, while the Holcrofts' decision was "understandable and very admirable", there was little evidence that such shock tactics change behaviour.

Statistics from the national crime survey suggest that the number of ecstasy users rose from 9% of 16-29-year-olds in 1996, the year after Leah Bett's death, to 12% in 2000, the last available figure, while heroin use doubled to 2%.

DrugScope's chief executive, Roger Howard, said: "We hope the image will succeed in changing government policy and encouraging more investment in treatment and harm reduction initiatives."

Chapter 4 | **Challenge 25**

Analysis of the newspaper article

The following people are quoted using direct or indirect speech

- Pauline Holcroft (mother of Rachael Whitear)
- Mick Holcroft (father of Rachael Whitear)
- Some drugs specialists
- Paul Betts (father of Leah Betts who died from taking Ecstasy)
- Rosie Brocklehurst (from drug treatment charity *Addiction*)
- Lynn Clare (project manager of the support group *Parents Against Drug Abuse*)
- Hertfordshire Local Education Authority
- *Drug scope* (drugs charity)
- Roger Howard (*Drugscope* Chief executive)

As you can see the article has been very well researched, with the writer ensuring that all relevant interest groups have had their views expressed. Sarah Hall uses both direct and reported speech in this article. In the following task you need to find quotes from the relevant sources, comment on whether they are direct or reported speech and comment on which side of the discussion is being presented.

Speaker	Quotes	Direct or reported?	What are they arguing? What effect does it have on the reader?
Pauline Holcroft			
Mick Holcroft			
Some drugs specialists			
Paul Betts			
Rosie Brocklehurst (from drug treatment charity Addiction)			
Lynn Clare (project manager of the support group Parents Against Drug Abuse)			
Hertfordshire Local Education Authority			
Drug scope (drugs charity)			
Roger Howard (Drugscope Chief executive)			

In what other subjects could I apply these skills?

Chapter 4 — Challenge 26

Challenge the teacher

a) Read through the following questions and revise them so that they are easier to understand.
b) Choose 3 possible answers for each question (one of them being the correct one!)
c) Swap your questions and multiple choice answers with your learning

1. What is the significant difference between using direct or reported speech? What impact is there on the reader? Use evidence from the article.
2. Pick out the use of emotive and disturbing language that the article uses in the first two paragraphs. What is the effect of these words? Why do you think Sarah Hall includes this section at the beginning of the article?
3. Comment on the use of facts and statistics in the article. Why have these been used? What impact might these facts have on the reader's opinion on whether the photograph should have been released?
4. Comment on why you think the writer included so many different sources. Why does she not give a personal opinion on such an emotive issue?
5. What are your opinions on the release of the photograph? Has the article in anyway changed your views? Give reasons for your answer.

Use of structure in newspaper articles

Read through the article on the next page and consider the way the information has been structured effectively for the reader.

- Dramatic opening headline to capture reader's attention
- Sums up the main points of interest in the article in opening paragraph
- Development of the story
- Use of supporting evidence
- Personal responses to what occurred
- Use of facts
- Use of dramatic and emotive vocabulary
- Police comment on the issue
- Further explanation
- View from the experts
- Background information about the case
- Final comment and update, with details of any future events surrounding the story

What has helped me learn effectively today?

Chapter 4

SO CLOSE TO A REAL DISASTER

Exclusive By Stephen Moyes

A SECRET report has revealed how close shoe bomber Richard Reid came to downing a jet and killing 197 passengers.

An email, leaked to The Daily Mirror, confirms for the first time how Reid's plan only failed as he used a single match to try to light the bomb's fuse.

If he had used a cigarette lighter or several matches the bomb in his trainer would have been detonated.

The confidential report reveals:

The amount and type of explosive would have downed the jet and sent "a lot of bodies flying through the sky".

Armed security staff were so alarmed by Reid's behavior they escorted him to his seat on the plane.

Airport staff were alarmed at Reid's body odour after he had spent the night in a four-star hotel.

Reid's luggage contained just two magazines, a radio, a cassette player and five Arabic cassettes, including two of verses from the Koran.

Reid, 29, was held by air crew and passengers after a stewardess spotted him trying to light the fuse in his shoe on American Airlines Flight 63 from Paris to Miami on December 22 last year.

Police in Boston, to where the plane was diverted after the in-flight terror, wrote to the head of America's security immediately after the incident.

They said igniting such an explosive "is generally achieved by a military M-60 or a commercial grade igniter. Time fuses can be split and by using several match heads, this can cause ignition."

Reid's shoes contained a trigger of highly unstable TATP - triacetone triperoxide - nicknamed Mother of Satan by Middle Eastern terrorists. This meant he needed no wires and batteries - parts likely to be spotted by airport checks.

The email said: "This TATP is reported to have been homemade. The detonating cord was then connected to the main charge - about 4oz of PETN in each shoe." PETN - pentaerythritoltetranitrate - is one of the most powerful high explosives.

Civil Aviation Security Editor for Jane's Publications Chris Yates said: "That amount in a pressurised tube of an aircraft would at the very least take out a window or panel. And that would result in an explosive decompression.

"Everything not strapped down would be sucked out as the hole in the window or paneling got bigger. It would result in a lot of bodies flying though the sky. Effectively it would down the airliner."

Reid, who had an authentic British passport issued in Brussels on December 7 2001, spent the night before his flight at a hotel. He was taken there by French police after being barred from boarding a plane on December 21.

The next day police decided they had no reason to detain him.

He had a ticket for a round trip via Miami and Antigua, where he told officers he intended to visit his family. He explained his lack of luggage by saying he had clothes at his family's home in the West Indies.

Before boarding the plane, the email said, Reid was screened and searched by the same agents as the previous day. They then escorted him to his seat.

The email said: "Despite having spent the night at the airport hotel, agents stated that the passenger smelt of body odour as if had not washed for some time."

The FBI believes the bomb shows a knowledge of explosives beyond Reid's abilities. It was reminiscent of those used by Palestinian suicide bombers, but more sophisticated, they say.

Reid faces at least five life sentences under America's Anti-Terrorism Bill, updated after the September 11 attacks.

Chapter 4

Using the conventions of a newspaper report for my own writing

The article uses many techniques in order to present the story in a factual and dramatic way. It is able to appeal to the needs of the target audience by providing facts and opinions as well as supporting evidence on the case.

Journalists have to research their story in great detail before writing as well as carefully selecting relevant information to ensure that they present a balanced view of events, which has supporting accounts of those involved.

Over the next few pages is an example of how you can write an effective newspaper article.

Chapter 4

Read all about it!
Writing an effective newspaper article

Elements	Explanation	Example
Dramatic opening headline to capture your reader's attention	This could be a simple word (or words) used for effect.	*DEVASTATED* *BURNED ALIVE!*
	It could be a rhetorical question to draw the reader in.	*Why did they all have to die?*
	It could use alliteration to increase its appeal:	*Teenager Torments Town*
	It could use a pun:	*FAT people weighing down the health service*
Opening paragraph that sums up the main points of the story	When it happened:	*Last night*
	Who was involved?	*two men*
	What happened?	*were arrested on suspicion of murder*
	Where did it happen?	*in Burnage, Manchester*
	Why did it happen?	*after DNA evidence linked the youths to last month's murder of a young girl from Stockport.*
Development of the story and background information	Greater detail of the incident is included here. Names of people involved etc.	*Simon Smith from Longsight and Tony Rogers from Withington are being accused of murdering Alison Burke after she came back from a night-club in Manchester's city centre last month. Since then a manhunt has been underway to track down the killer or killers who stabbed the 25-year-old law student who should have been completing her qualifications next month. When news broke of her killing last month, it rocked the local community who were devastated by the tragic loss of such a popular girl.*

Chapter 4

Read all about it!
Writing an effective newspaper article

Elements	Explanation	Example
Responses from people involved in the story **Either direct speech or reported speech.** **Direct speech –** the actual words spoken therefore quotation marks needed. **Reported speech –** a summary of what was said – not the actual words – therefore no quotation marks needed)	This could be the police /experts: (direct speech)	*Inspector Regan who is leading the investigation said: "This is a major breakthrough in the investigation though enquiries are still on-going"*
	An eye-witness (direct speech)	*One on-looker, who did not want to be named commented: "They were trying to escape by the back of my shop – I was scared to death – thankfully the police arrived in time, otherwise I doubt if I would be here talking to you now"*
	Relatives/friends of the people involved. Reported speech	*On hearing of the men's arrest, the victim's father, John Burke said that he was relieved and hoped that justice would finally be done.*
	People representing the people accused (direct speech)	*The solicitor, Mr. Knight, who is representing the two men accused said: "Both of my clients categorically deny this charge"*
Final comment and update on the story	This could be the time of a trial/police statement/sentence given etc.	*The two men will be questioned further this evening and are expected to be at Stockport Magistrates on Thursday morning.*

Chapter 4 — Challenge 27

Using the techniques on the previous pages, write your own article on a topical issue of your choice.

Read all about it!
Writing an effective newspaper article

What strategies could I use to progress further?

Elements	Explanation	Your response
Dramatic opening headline to capture your reader's attention	This could be a simple word (or words) used for effect.	
	It could be a rhetorical question to draw the reader in.	
	It could use alliteration to increase its appeal:	
	It could use a pun:	
Opening paragraph that sums up the main points of the story	When it happened:	
	Who was involved?	
	What happened?	
	Where did it happen?	
	Why did it happen?	
Development of the story and background information	Greater detail of the incident is included here.	
	Names of people involved etc.	

144

Chapter 4

Read all about it!
Writing an effective newspaper article

Elements	Explanation	Your response
Responses from people involved in the story **Either direct speech or reported speech.** **Direct speech – the actual words spoken therefore quotation marks needed.** **Reported speech – a summary of what was said – not the actual words – therefore no quotation marks needed)**	This could be the police /experts: (direct speech)	
	An eye-witness (direct speech)	
	Relatives/friends of the people involved. Reported speech	
	People representing the people accused (direct speech)	
Final comment and update on the story	This could be the time of a trial/police statement/sentence given etc.	

145

Chapter 4

Using effective headlines and presentational features in a newspaper report

Below are a collection of the front pages from The Mirror newspaper during the war in Iraq.

Challenge 28

In a small group, discuss how the following features are used and consider what impact these front pages would have on the public.

Use of headlines/ Sub-headings	Capitals	Rhetorical Questions	Use of alliteration
Choice of font	Photographs	Emotive Language	Presentation of the troops
Underlining	Captions	Sentence variation	Presentation of the politicians

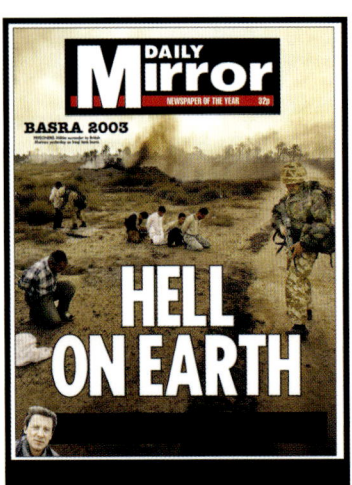

When could I use these skills outside of school?

Chapter 4   **Challenge 29**

Reporting on a sporting/music event

In threes, choose any sport/music event that you are familiar with and discuss a recent big occasion. (big game/live concert etc.)
A&B discuss the game
C records the main parts of their conversation
C now needs to ask further questions of the event in order to produce a plan for a report.

You may wish to refer to the opening of this sports report for advice on layout and structure

---

Manchester United 1
Manchester City 2
Derby double for Sven

David McDonnell 11/02/2008

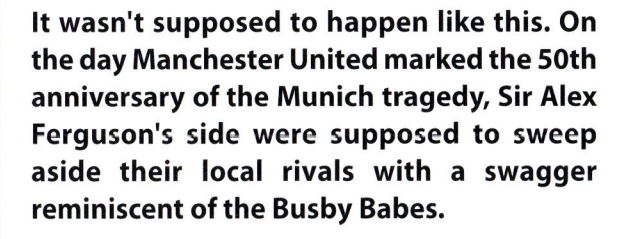

It wasn't supposed to happen like this. On the day Manchester United marked the 50th anniversary of the Munich tragedy, Sir Alex Ferguson's side were supposed to sweep aside their local rivals with a swagger reminiscent of the Busby Babes.

Manchester City were cast in the role of obliging opponents who would turn up and fulfil their duty as cannon fodder for the Premier League champions on an emotional afternoon at Old Trafford which remembered the 23 who died in Munich.

Instead Sven Goran Eriksson inspired City to their first win at Old Trafford since 1974, when Denis Law's back-heel condemned his former club to relegation, and their first League double over United since 1970.

Shaping your ideas in advertising

When asked to write an advert for a particular product (it could be your own invention) it is vitally important that you have a clear sense of

- who your target audience are
- what are their needs
- type of market you are aiming at (universal/specialist/bargain hunters/top range)
- what is your unique selling point (how are you different from the rest?)
- price
- methods of advertising (radio/tv/newspaper/web page/ poster)
- timing
- slogan
- layout of information

In what other subjects could I apply these skills?

Chapter 4

Watch an advert on TV, listen to one on the radio and read one in a newspaper.

Think about:

a) What is it trying to achieve?
b) What devices does it use?
c) How effectively does it do this?
d) How would its target audience react to this advert?
e) What would you have done differently to have a greater impact on your target audience?

The following web page forms part of Manchester's tourism board.

Challenge 30

a) in pairs read the web pages and discuss what you would change (and why)
b) produce your own web page, in which you advertise your own town/village.

Uniquely Manchester

visit manchester

Inviting, original, edgy, happening, different: spend any time in Manchester and you'll soon see it's a place like no other. This free-spirited city demands your attention with a warm, no-nonsense welcome and a liberating open-mindedness that challenges you to take part. Bring us your ideas, your energy and your attitude and you'll fit right in – that's what makes our city uniquely Manchester....

Bolton: there's a new trail in town…
Discover Bolton's inventors, presenters, crackerjacks and steeplejacks.

Cityscapes
Manchester is a dramatic mix of old and new. The futuristic design and innovative shapes of its contemporary architecture sit side by side with the spires and grinning gargoyles of its proud past

Manchester Industrial Heritage
Manchester was the trail-blazing spirit behind the Industrial Revolution of the 18th and 19th centuries, which led the world into the modern industrial era. Transport yourself back in time with the fascinating legacy of a period that changed the way we live.

What has helped me learn effectively today?

Chapter 4

Uniquely Manchester

visit manchester

Manchester Music
Manchester is one of the world's most innovative, original and exciting places for both making music and going out to listen to it. Here you can have it all: follow in the footsteps of Morrissey, look out for the next Happy Mondays or Oasis, enjoy world-class classical performances, or club it like there's no tomorrow…

Manchester People
The people of Manchester have an attitude to life and a way of doing things all their own. We're an easy, self-deprecating lot with a wicked sense of humour and an appetite for adventure (and a party). But don't be fooled: behind that engaging, easy-going exterior there lies ambition and desire for change. Here we celebrate the people of Manchester, and the things they've said and done.

Future Skills – using sources effectively

You are interested in gaining some work experience as a newspaper reporter and have to prepare the following as part of the interview

If you were asked to write the following articles,

	What sources would you use? (who would you ask?)	What questions would you ask them?
The local primary school has had to be closed down due to an outbreak of severe food poisoning		
School bus drivers have gone on strike due to increase in violent incidents against them		
Y10 girl is called up to Olympic squad		

Chapter 4

Personalised Progression

Assessment Focus 4 – construct paragraphs and use cohesion within and between paragraphs

How is my work at KS3 assessed?

Your work is assessed using assessment focuses which help you and your teacher determine what level your work is currently at. This criteria is often used when assessing your APP work and other classroom assessments. In this unit we will be looking at how to progress in AF4 (see above)

Key questions:
- What level am I currently working at in this assessment focus for writing? (if unsure, ask your English teacher)
- What skills do I currently have in this assessment focus?
- What skills do I need to develop to get to the next level?

In this section, you will be completing a series of challenges which will show you how you can personally progress to the next level, using many of the skills that you have developed in this unit.

How can I practice my skills to reach the next level in this assessment focus?

In this assessment focus (AF4), if you are currently working at...

Level 3	**go to Progress Checker A (Level 3-4 progression)**
Level 4	**go to Progress Checker B (Level 4-5 progression)**
Level 5	**go to Progress Checker C (Level 5-6 progression)**
Level 6	**go to Progress Checker D (Level 6-7 progression)**

When you get to the stage where you feel that you are confident in a particular level in this assessment focus, you can attempt the challenges for the next level.

Chapter 4

Progress Checker A – (Level 3-4 writing progression)

\multicolumn{3}{	l	}{**Assessment Focus 4** – construct paragraphs and use cohesion within and between paragraphs}
1	What level am I currently working at in AF4 writing?	Level 3
2	What skills do I currently have in this assessment focus?	As a Level 3 writer in AF4 I am able to: • loosely organise my ideas using a paragraph/section within a text; • make some links between sentences within paragraphs/sections; • move between paragraphs/sections though this is often disjointed
3	What skills do I need to develop to reach the next level?	To be a confident AF4 writer at Level 4 I need to • use paragraphs/sections to help organise my content • Use simple connectives to make links between sentences, within paragraphs/sections • attempt to establish simple links between paragraphs/sections

AF4 Progress Challenge
Moving a Level 3 response to Level 4

1) The table below includes a Level 3 response in AF4. Look at how this pupil has achieved this level and think about what they could do to improve.

Write a newspaper article about a disaster in your local town.

AF4 – Level 3 response	Why the pupils achieved a Level 3
Boy drowns when skating on the ice Tom Smith drowned yesterday when he went through the ice. They fought they could save him but he died. They said he was just having fun when he slipped through the ice and drowned.	Ideas are loosely organised into sections: headline – opening section – more information. Some links are made between sentences and paragraphs 'they' though this is unclear for the reader.

Chapter 4

How could we move this response into Level 4?

AF4 – Level 3 response	AF4 – Level 4 response
Boy drowns when skating on the ice Tom Smith drowned yesterday when he went through the ice. They fought they could save him but he died. They said he was just having fun when he slipped through the ice and drowned.	*Boys drowns in local lake after falling through ice* A young boy from Stockport, Tom Smith drowned yesterday after skating on the icy pond. ==People passing by== and the doctors thought they could save him but it was too late. ==Witnesses told police== that he was laughing one minute then he was gone.

Notice how the Level 4 response

- Elaborates on the main idea by adding an extra explanation that is relevant
- Makes appropriate links between sentences (people passing by) and paragraphs (Witnesses told police)

Next steps…

- Make sure that each paragraph has a topic sentence and a connecting points which explains what is occurring in each paragraph
- Link each sentence so that they help to present your point of view
- Start to a new paragraph when there is a change in time/place/event/topic/speaker.

Chapter 4

Progress Checker B – (Level 4-5 writing progression)

	Assessment Focus 4 – construct paragraphs and use cohesion within and between paragraphs	
1	What level am I currently working at in AF4 writing?	Level 4
2	What skills do I currently have in this assessment focus?	As a Level 4 writer in AF4 I am able to: • use paragraphs/sections to help organise my content • use simple connectives to make links between sentences, within paragraphs/sections • attempt to establish simple links between paragraphs/sections
3	What skills do I need to develop to reach the next level?	To be a confident AF4 writer at Level 5 I need to • use paragraphs to clearly structure main ideas across a text to support my purpose; • use a range of devices to support cohesion within paragraphs/sections; • make links between paragraphs/sections across the whole text.

AF4 Progress Challenge
Moving a Level 4 response to Level 5

The table below includes a Level 4 response in AF4. Look at how this pupil has achieved this level and think about what they could do to improve.

AF4 – Level 4 response	Why the pupils achieved a Level 4
A young boy from Stockport, Tom Smith drowned yesterday after skating on the icy pond. People passing by and the doctors thought they could save him but it was too late. Witnesses told police that he was laughing one minute then he was gone.	• Elaborates on the main idea by adding an extra explanation that is relevant • Makes appropriate links between sentences (people passing by) and paragraphs (Witnesses told police)

Chapter 4

How could we move this response into Level 5?

AF4 – Level 4 response	AF4 – Level 5 response
A young boy from Stockport, Tom Smith drowned yesterday after skating on the icy pond. People passing by and the doctors thought they could save him but it was too late. Witnesses told police that he was laughing one minute then he was gone.	Devastated parents of Stockport teenager, Tom Smith, were yesterday being comforted by relatives after discovering that their thirteen year old son had drowned, after ice skating in Bramhall Park. Tom, from Hazel Grove, was believed to have got into danger when thin ice cracked under his feet. Passers-by tried to help though could not get to the boy in time.

Notice how the Level 5 response

- clearly uses paragraphs to support the main idea (story of the boy)
- uses a reference back to the text to link the paragraphs (Tom, from Hazel Grove) and the sentences within paragraphs (Passers-by tried to help)

Next steps…

- Make sure that within each paragraph, there is a reference chain to the previous point made.

Chapter 4

Progress Checker C – (Level 5-6 writing progression)

	Assessment Focus 4 – construct paragraphs and use cohesion within and between paragraphs	
1	What level am I currently working at in AF4 writing?	Level 5
2	What skills do I currently have in this assessment focus?	As a Level 5 writer in AF4 I am able to: • use paragraphs to clearly structure main ideas across a text to support my purpose; • use a range of devices to support cohesion within paragraphs/sections; • make links between paragraphs/sections across the whole text.
3	What skills do I need to develop to reach the next level?	To be a confident AF4 writer at Level 6 I need to • construct paragraphs clearly to supports meaning and purpose; • use cohesive devices within paragraphs to contribute to emphasis and effect.

AF4 Progress Challenge
Moving a Level 5 response to Level 6

The table below includes a Level 5 response in AF4. Look at how this pupil has achieved this level and think about what they could do to improve.

AF4 – Level 5 response	Why the pupils achieved a Level 5
Devastated parents of Stockport teenager, Tom Smith, were yesterday being comforted by relatives after discovering that their thirteen year old son had drowned, after ice skating in Bramhall Park. Tom, from Hazel Grove, was believed to have got into danger when thin ice cracked under his feet. Passers-by tried to help though could not get to the boy in time.	• clearly uses paragraphs to support the main idea (story of the boy) • uses a reference back to the text to link the paragraphs (Tom, from Hazel Grove) and the sentences within paragraphs (Passers-by tried to help)

Chapter 4

How could we move this response into Level 6?

AF4 – Level 5 response	AF4 – Level 6 response
Devastated parents of Stockport teenager, Tom Smith, were yesterday being comforted by relatives after discovering that their thirteen year old son had drowned, after ice skating in Bramhall Park. Tom, from Hazel Grove, was believed to have got into danger when thin ice cracked under his feet. Passers-by tried to help though could not get to the boy in time.	Devastated parents of Stockport teenager, Tom Smith, were yesterday being comforted by relatives after discovering that their thirteen year old son had drowned, after ice skating in Bramhall Park. What started out as a bit of fun in the snowy weather, turned into a day of disaster. Tom, from Hazel Grove, was believed to have got into danger when thin ice cracked under his feet though no one could help him. Frantically trying to rescue him, passer-by Simon Hughes, said the whole community was in shock.

Notice how the Level 6 response

- Constructs paragraphs for effect
- Varies paragraph length for effect.
- Uses a range of features to link sentences and paragraphs (beginning sentence with an adverb 'frantically')

Next steps…

- For every paragraph you write, produce and complete two columns:
  1) meaning 2) purpose
- Between each paragraphs, use reference chains to link with previous content
- Use adverbial phrases to begin paragraphs to draw your reader in.

Chapter 4

Progress Checker D – (Level 6-7 writing progression)

	Assessment Focus 4 – construct paragraphs and use cohesion within and between paragraphs	
1	What level am I currently working at in AF4 writing?	Level 6
2	What skills do I currently have in this assessment focus?	As a Level 6 writer in AF4 I am able to: • construct paragraphs clearly to support meaning and purpose; • use cohesive devices within paragraphs to contribute to emphasis and effect.
3	What skills do I need to develop to reach the next level?	To be a confident AF4 writer at Level 7 I need to • ensure that paragraphing across the text is integral to meaning and purpose; • shape or craft individual paragraphs for imaginative or rhetorical effect.

AF4 Progress Challenge
Moving a Level 6 response to Level 7

The table below includes a Level 6 response in AF4. Look at how this pupil has achieved this level and think about what they could do to improve.

AF4 – Level 6 response	Why the pupils achieved a Level 6
Devastated parents of Stockport teenager, Tom Smith, were yesterday being comforted by relatives after discovering that their thirteen year old son had drowned, after ice skating in Bramhall Park. What started out as a bit of fun in the snowy weather, turned into a day of disaster. Tom, from Hazel Grove, was believed to have got into danger when thin ice cracked under his feet though no one could help him. Frantically trying to rescue him, passer-by Simon Hughes, said the whole community was in shock.	• Constructs paragraphs for effect • Varies paragraph length for effect. • Uses a range of features to link sentences and paragraphs (beginning sentence with an adverb 'frantically')

Chapter 4

How could we move this response into Level 7?

AF4 – Level 6 response	AF4 – Level 7 response
Devastated parents of Stockport teenager, Tom Smith, were yesterday being comforted by relatives after discovering that their thirteen year old son had drowned, after ice skating in Bramhall Park. *What started out as a bit of fun in the snowy weather, turned into a day of disaster.* *Tom, from Hazel Grove, was believed to have got into danger when thin ice cracked under his feet though no one could help him.* *Frantically trying to rescue him, passer-by Simon Hughes, said the whole community was in shock.*	How many more of our children will be killed until the public realise the dangers of icy lakes? What started out as a bit of fun in the snowy weather for a family from Hazel Grove, turned into a catastrophic tragedy, leading to the death of a thirteen year old boy. Tom, from Hazel Grove, was believed to have got into danger when thin ice cracked under his feet though no one could help him. "It's a devastating blow to the family, and our community", agonised Simon Hughes, who tried, in vain, to save the boy.

Notice how the Level 7 response

- Uses the construction of paragraphs to support the meaning of the article (and the writer's purpose and voice in expressing the sheer tragedy of the event)
- Use of rhetorical techniques to impact on the reader "How many more…"

Next steps…

- Use a variety of cohesive devices to link your paragraphs, such as adverbial phrases, rhetorical questions etc.
- Make sure that individual paragraphs have their own particular purpose in supporting your overall meaning
- Place different paragraph types and lengths next to each other (juxtaposition) to achieve different effects.

Chapter 5 — Rights, Candour, Action

Programme of Study Links	**Critical understanding** - exploring others' ideas and developing your own Analysing and evaluating spoken and written language to appreciate how meaning is shaped
Framework Objectives	**8.1b** developing own viewpoint, drawing on evidence, opinions and the particular purpose of the task **8.3** improving vocabulary for precision and impact **8.4** developing varied linguistic and literary techniques
Personal Learning & Thinking Skills	Independent enquirers – identify questions to answer and problems to solve Team workers – providing constructive support and feedback to others
AFL	Exploring success criteria Developing questioning techniques Peer and self assessment
Assessment Focus	AF3 – produce texts which are appropriate to task, reader and purpose AF7 – select appropriate and effective vocabulary
Functional Skills	Communicating ideas and opinions, effectively and persuasively

What has helped me learn effectively today?

Challenge 1 - Get thinking

In pairs, respond verbally to the following phrases and consider,
1) Where they may have come from?
2) Why they have been written.
3) Who they may be aimed at?

1. **Yes we can!**

2. **Diana was the very essence of compassion, of duty, of style, of beauty.**

3. **Of course teenagers love to wear the cardboard shirts, the old fashioned blazers, and those, oh so nice, awkward fitting trousers. Who in their right mind would want to wear their own, more comfortable clothes to school when sitting behind a desk all day?**

4. **Any form of suicide is devastating for the people left behind.**

5. **I experienced it watching matches in the stands as well. I was about 13 and my friend managed to get some tickets and we were sitting enjoying the game.**

6. **500 bucks is quite a lot for a console. But you will be getting the best of the best. With all the great technology and games, £299.99 is cheap.**

Chapter 5

In this unit I will learn how to effectively… *(Learning Objectives)*	**8.1b** developing own viewpoint, drawing on evidence, opinions and the particular purpose of the task **8.3** improving vocabulary for precision and impact **8.4** developing varied linguistic and literary techniques
The topics I will be studying are… *(Stimulus)*	• Speech writing • Reviews • Commentaries
My understand will be checked by seeing how I… *(Assessment Criteria)*	AF2 - produce texts which are appropriate to task, reader and purpose AF7 - select appropriate and effective vocabulary
My achievement will be demonstrated through me successfully completing the following challenges: *(Learning Outcomes)*	1) Get thinking – language challenge 2) Experimenting with vocabulary 3) Confidence levels task 4) Adverb adventure 5) Simile games 6) Developing similes 7) Diagnosis Dialogue 8) Language speculation 9) Finding your own voice 10) Speech analysis 11) Analysis of Bill Clinton's speech 12) Writing a persuasive speech 13) Analysis of emotive speech 14) Description of someone 'close' 15) Own speech writing 16) Analysis of Euthanasia commentary 17) Considering humour use 18) Soap Opera analysis 19) Responding to an article on race 20) How are you inspired by Jay Z? 21) Discussing a review 22) Editing a review of PS3 and Wii 23) Writing a film review 24) Analysis of book reviews 25) Writing own book review 26) Responding to a provocative statement Future skills – exploring school rules

Chapter 5

Rights, Candour, Action

Developing viewpoint, voice and ideas in non-fiction

In this chapter we are looking at how you can communicate your thoughts which allows the reader to understand that you have a right to express your opinion with candour (in an open and direct way) which will often require your audience to take action. Writers, and particularly speech writers, will use a variety of language devices in an attempt to impact on their audience and achieve their purpose. This type of writing should have a particular individual and personalised tone, especially as it is focusing on reflecting on a topic and actively involving your reader.

Below are some of the features that you would expect to find in this type of writing.		
Sentence structure and punctuation	**Text Structure and Organisation**	**Composition and effect**
Topic sentences will be used to highlight specific areas of discussion. Subordination and coordination I used effectively to express points in a clear and imaginative way. Rhetorical questions are used to appeal directly to the reader and have a dramatic effect. 1st or 3rd person will be used – depending on the purpose and target audience. Variety of sentence types will be used in order to appeal to the reader	Title is catchy and reveals purpose to the reader. Opening sections often provide a brief summary of what is to be discussed Points are supported in each paragraph by including relevant detail. Comparisons may be used in order to help with explaining points. A clear structure will be included when analysing a topic or text in order to clarify points and arrive at a clear conclusion. Length of paragraphs will vary according to the purpose. Short paragraphs may be used when providing a concise review. When commenting on a topic the paragraphs should be organised to help structure the thought processes. A concluding paragraph will summarise the main points of the writing task	Tone will vary according to the purpose and target audience. Vocabulary will be sophisticated and ambitious. Tenses will be consistent Adjectives and adverbs will be used regularly to add emphasis to the writing Formal or informal language will be applied where necessary. Appealing directly to the reader will be a main feature of this writing.

Chapter 5

Wise Words – developing your vocabulary

You have probably often been asked to 'extend' or 'develop' or 'improve' your vocabulary.

Whilst using a dictionary/thesaurus obviously helps, you must also ensure that vocabulary chosen:

- is in the correct context;
- adds to the meaning you are wanting to get across to the reader; (not just chosen because it seems like a 'big' word)
- will help you achieve your purpose;
- is placed carefully within the sentence for maximum effect.

Challenge 2

Read through the list of words below which could be used as prepositions. In pairs, you need to read out a sentence which begins with each preposition. (take turns)

about	behind	from	over	till
above	below	in	pace	times
across	beneath	inside	past	to
adjacent	beside	into	per	towards
after	between	like	plus	under
against	beyond	near	regarding	unlike
along	despite	next	round	until
among	down	of	save	up
around	during	on	since	versus
aside	except	opposite	than	with
barring	failing	out	through	within
before	following	outside	throughout	without

In what other subjects could I apply these skills?

Chapter 5 — Challenge 3

Below are some examples of the type of changes you could make to your vocabulary use. Look through these and rate each one, based on how confident you feel as in using them: (1 highly confident – 5 no confidence)

Features of effective vocabulary	From…	To…
Reducing the amount of pronoun use	She went to the shops then she decided to go home because she was feeling poorly	The frail teenager went to the shops then decided to go home because of feeling poorly.
Develop use of adverbs to give extra meaning to a verb, adjective, another adverb or complete sentence	I walked back from the shops It was a good party though rubbish food	I frantically walked back from the shops. It was a fairly good party though really rubbish food.
Increase adjective use to describe something in a more powerful, imaginative way.	It was a cold night and I wanted to be back at my house in front of the fire.	It was an arctic night and I wanted to be back at my sizzling fire.
Using prepositions effectively to add more detail	The bag lay abandoned and forgotten under the floorboards	Under the floorboards, the bag lay abandoned
Use of: alliteration	Fred decided to leave quickly otherwise he would have been caught shoplifting again.	Fred flew out of the shop, fearful of being caught shoplifting again.
similes	She felt lonely looking out of her window.	She was as lonely as a lighthouse, staring out at the empty sea.
metaphor	Her eyes were blue and shiny when she looked at me.	Her eyes were blue diamonds, sparking intently at me.
personification	I felt jealous and wanted to get her back.	Jealousy raged inside me, toying with my sense, daring me to take revenge.
Assonance	Get warm and reduce your pain	Feel the warmth, heal the pain.
Use of puns (particular in headlines)	Wayne Rooney was sent off in Spain last night in the pouring rain	THE WAYNE IN SPAIN IS A PAIN.

What strategies could I use to progress further?

Chapter 5 — Challenge 4

When could I use these skills outside of school?

Adverb Adventure

In a group, read through the list of words below which could all be used as an adverb.
a) decide which ones you are familiar with
b) for the ones that you are not, look up in a dictionary
c) As a group, compile 10 sentences in which a range of the adverbs you were initially unfamiliar with are used. The sentences need to be linked in some way so there is a narrative (story) created.

- accidentally angrily anxiously awkwardly
- badly blindly boastfully boldly bravely briefly brightly busily
- calmly carefully carelessly cautiously cheerfully clearly correctly courageously
- crossly crucially cruelly
- daily defiantly deliberately doubtfully
- easily elegantly enormously enthusiastically equally
- faithfully fatally fearfully fiercely fondly foolishly fortunately frantically
- gently gladly gracefully greedily
- happily hastily honestly hungrily
- innocently inquisitively irritably
- joyously justly jokingly jerkily
- kindly kinaesthetically
- lazily loudly languidly laudably laughably
- madly merrily mortally mysteriously
- nearly neatly nervously noisily nicely
- obediently obnoxiously
- painfully perfectly politely poorly powerfully promptly punctually
- quickly quietly quintessentially
- rapidly rarely really recklessly regularly reluctantly repeatedly rightfully
- roughly rudely
- sadly safely seldom selfishly seriously shakily sharply shyly silently sleepily
- slowly smoothly softly solemnly speedily sternly successfully suddenly
- surreptitiously suspiciously swiftly
- tenderly tensely thoughtfully tightly truthfully
- unexpectedly undoubtedly universally
- victoriously violently vivaciously vociferously
- warmly weakly wearily wildly waywardly
- xenophobically
- yearningly
- zealously

Chapter 5

Challenge 5

Playing around with similes

For this challenge, you need to improve and extend the following sentence, using the list of words below (or your own choices) . Go for ambitious, funny and unexpected combinations rather than the obvious choices such as 'as cold as ice'; as green as grass'

He was as funny as an undertaker who lives for nothing else.

> **angelic agile bald big bold brave bright busy cool careful cold crafty careless cautious clear clean calm cunning crazy cute drunk dry dull dreary easy elegant fresh funny gentle happy insensitive insecure high hot hungry keen mad merry modest pale patient pretty proud pure quick scared sensitive slippery smooth soft solid sour sound steady sticky stiff straight strong stubborn sturdy sure timid tough tricky understated welcome wise xenophobic zealous**

Challenge 6

Developing your similes use

Choose your five favourite similes and change into a metaphor/personification

For example:
Her actions were as brave as a soldier, who puts their country first

To: Bravery seeped out of every pour

What has helped me learn effectively today?

In what other subjects could I apply these skills?

Chapter 5 — Challenge 7

What strategies could I use to progress further?

Diagnosis Dialogue

Using vocabulary effectively when describing speech.

a) Read through the paragraph below and think about what is the common feature that needs improving:

"Stop that!" said Terry.
"I wish that you would stop blaming me for everything" said Tom
"Who was it then?" said Terry
"It was you - I saw you" said Tom.

Yawn, yawn yawn!

It is vitally important that when using dialogue that you signal to your reader the emotions that the characters are feeling during their speech. This can be structured in a variety of ways:

Using more exciting verbs to describe the dialogue (after the speech)	"Stop that!" screamed Terry
Introduction of the character's feelings before and after the speech	Terry shouted back at Tom, "Stop that!" with anger running through his veins
Use of an adverb to further inform the reader of the way the character was feeling.	"I wish that you would stop blaming me for everything" replied Tom, dejectedly

b) Read through a piece of writing you have recently completed which included dialogue. Think about how else you could describe your characters speech, using the techniques above. Remember that your choice of verbs and adverbs should be selected to reflect the context of your writing (how your characters' are feeling at that particular point).

Chapter 5 — Challenge 8

a) With your learning partner, read through the list of words below and discuss where they may have come from.
b) Choose 10 words from this list which you feel are the most powerful and explain why you think this.
c) Produce a paragraph using only the words from this list. (Your choice of 10).

achieve	energy	perfect	task
ahead	enormity	perfected	tomorrow
all	first	possible;	tonight
alliances	generation	power	touched
America	get	power	toward
answer	give	progress	true
began	God	promise	truly
believed	greatest	promote	truth
belongs	greatness	prosperity	union
bless	grew	rejected	united
block	Happen	Remaking	unyielding
brave	hear	repair	yet
braved	heard	resolves	you
breathe	help	respond	your
brick	history	responsibility	us
bridge	honest	restore	victory
bright	hope	road	voice
bring	hopeful	service	voices
build	hopes	service,	volunteered
built	liberty	spirit	we
can	moment	sacrifice	will
cause	nation	saved	win
celebrate	need	seek	with
challenges	new	strength	work
chance	our	struggle	working
change	ourselves	suffers	world
climb	overcome	summon	yes
conquer	patriotism	sums	
democracy	peace	support	
enduring	people	save	

When could I use these skills outside of school?

167

Chapter 5

How to write an effective speech

You probably make great speeches without even realising it. From elaborate homework excuses to trying to explain why you need yet another top-up card for your mobile, it's a gift you are blessed with! In this section we are going to analyse what makes a great speech and how we can use these skills to develop your own voice when communicating effectively.

The following speech was given by President Barrack Obama on the night of his election victory. Consider how he uses language effectively to appeal to the American public.

If there is anyone out there who still doubts that America is a place where all things are possible; who still wonders if the dream of our founders is alive in our time; who still questions the power of our democracy, tonight is your answer.

It's the answer told by lines that stretched around schools and churches in numbers this nation has never seen; by people who waited three hours and four hours, many for the very first time in their lives, because they believed that this time must be different; that their voices could be that difference.

It's the answer spoken by young and old, rich and poor, Democrat and Republican, black, white, Hispanic, Asian, Native American, gay, straight, disabled and not disabled - Americans who sent a message to the world that we have never been just a collection of individuals or a collection of Red States and Blue States: we are, and always will be, the United States of America.

It's the answer that led those who have been told for so long by so many to be cynical, and fearful, and doubtful of what we can achieve to put their hands on the arc of history and bend it once more toward the hope of a better day. It's been a long time coming, but tonight, because of what we did on this day, in this election, at this defining moment, change has come to America.

VICTORY FOR THE PEOPLE

But above all, I will never forget who this victory truly belongs to - it belongs to you.

I was never the likeliest candidate for this office. We didn't start with much money or many endorsements. Our campaign was not hatched in the halls of Washington - it began in the backyards of Des Moines and the living rooms of Concord and the front porches of Charleston. It was built by working men and women who dug into what little savings they had to give $5 and $10 and $20 to the cause.

Chapter 5

It grew strength from the young people who rejected the myth of their generation's apathy; who left their homes and their families for jobs that offered little pay and less sleep; it grew strength from the not-so-young people who braved the bitter cold and scorching heat to knock on the doors of perfect strangers; from the millions of Americans who volunteered, and organised, and proved that more than two centuries later, a government of the people, by the people and for the people has not perished from the Earth. This is your victory.

THE TASK AHEAD

I know you didn't do this just to win an election and I know you didn't do it for me. You did it because you understand the enormity of the task that lies ahead. For even as we celebrate tonight, we know the challenges that tomorrow will bring are the greatest of our lifetime - two wars, a planet in peril, the worst financial crisis in a century.

Even as we stand here tonight, we know there are brave Americans waking up in the deserts of Iraq and the mountains of Afghanistan to risk their lives for us.

There are mothers and fathers who will lie awake after their children fall asleep and wonder how they'll make the mortgage, or pay their doctor's bills, or save enough for their child's college education. There is new energy to harness and new jobs to be created; new schools to build and threats to meet and alliances to repair.

REMAKING THE NATION

The road ahead will be long. Our climb will be steep. We may not get there in one year or even in one term, but America - I have never been more hopeful than I am tonight that we will get there. I promise you - we as a people will get there.

There will be setbacks and false starts. There are many who won't agree with every decision or policy I make as president, and we know that government can't solve every problem. But I will always be honest with you about the challenges we face. I will listen to you, especially when we disagree.

And above all, I will ask you to join in the work of remaking this nation the only way it's been done in America for 221 years - block by block, brick by brick, calloused hand by calloused hand.

ONE NATION, ONE PEOPLE

What began 21 months ago in the depths of winter cannot end on this autumn night. This victory alone is not the change we seek - it is only the chance for us to make that change. And that cannot happen if we go back to the way things were. It cannot happen without you, without a new spirit of service, a new spirit of sacrifice.

So let us summon a new spirit of patriotism; of service and responsibility where each of us resolves to pitch in and work harder and look after not only ourselves, but each other. Let us remember that if this financial crisis taught us anything, it's that we cannot have a thriving Wall Street while Main Street suffers - in this country, we rise or fall as one nation; as one people. And to those Americans whose support I have yet to earn - I may not have won your vote tonight, but I hear your voices, I need your help, and I will be your president too.

AMERICA IN THE WORLD

To those who would tear the world down - we will defeat you. To those who seek peace and security - we support you.

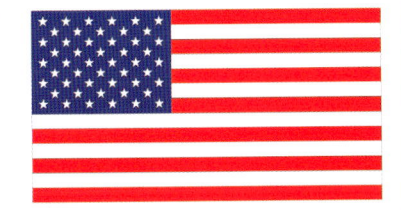

Chapter 5

And to all those who have wondered if America's beacon still burns as bright - tonight we proved once more that the true strength of our nation comes not from the might of our arms or the scale of our wealth, but from the enduring power of our ideals: democracy, liberty, opportunity and unyielding hope.

For that is the true genius of America - that America can change. Our union can be perfected. And what we have already achieved gives us hope for what we can and must achieve tomorrow.

A HISTORY OF STRUGGLE

This election had many firsts and many stories that will be told for generations. But one that's on my mind tonight is about a woman who cast her ballot in Atlanta. She's a lot like the millions of others who stood in line to make their voice heard in this election except for one thing - Ann Nixon Cooper is 106 years old.

She was born just a generation past slavery; a time when there were no cars on the road or planes in the sky; when someone like her couldn't vote for two reasons - because she was a woman and because of the colour of her skin.

And tonight, I think about all that she's seen throughout her century in America - the heartache and the hope; the struggle and the progress; the times we were told that we can't, and the people who pressed on with that American creed: Yes, we can.

At a time when women's voices were silenced and their hopes dismissed, she lived to see them stand up and speak out and reach for the ballot. Yes, we can.

When there was despair in the dust bowl and depression across the land, she saw a nation conquer fear itself with a New Deal, new jobs and a new sense of common purpose. Yes, we can.

When the bombs fell on our harbour and tyranny threatened the world, she was there to witness a generation rise to greatness and a democracy was saved. Yes, we can.

She was there for the buses in Montgomery, the hoses in Birmingham, a bridge in Selma, and a preacher from Atlanta who told a people that "we shall overcome". Yes, we can.

A man touched down on the Moon, a wall came down in Berlin, a world was connected by our own science and imagination. And this year, in this election, she touched her finger to a screen, and cast her vote, because after 106 years in America, through the best of times and the darkest of hours, she knows how America can change. Yes, we can.

THIS IS OUR MOMENT

America, we have come so far. We have seen so much. But there is so much more to do. So tonight, let us ask ourselves - if our children should live to see the next century; if my daughters should be so lucky to live as long as Ann Nixon Cooper, what change will they see? What progress will we have made?

This is our chance to answer that call. This is our moment.

This is our time - to put our people back to work and open doors of opportunity for our kids; to restore prosperity and promote the cause of peace; to reclaim the American dream and reaffirm that fundamental truth - that out of many, we are one; that while we breathe, we hope, and where we are met with cynicism and doubt, and those who tell us that we can't, we will respond with that timeless creed that sums up the spirit of a people: yes, we can.

Thank you, God bless you, and may God bless the United States of America.

Chapter 5

How Obama uses a variety of linguistic and literary techniques

Below are some examples of the language devices used by the President to reassure the American people that the change he promised during the election will be realised now that he has been elected.

If there is anyone out there **who still** doubts that America is a place where all things are possible; **who still** wonders if the dream of our founders is alive in our time; **who still** questions the power of our democracy, tonight is your answer.	**Use or repetition for dramatic effect** **Power of three**
It's the answer told by lines that stretched around schools and churches in numbers this nation has never seen; by people who waited three hours and four hours, many for the very first time in their lives, because they believed that this time must be different; that their voices could be that difference.	
It's the answer spoken by young and old, rich and poor, Democrat and Republican, black, white, Hispanic, Asian, Native American, gay, straight, disabled and not disabled - Americans who sent a message to the world that we have never been just a collection of individuals or a collection of Red States and Blue States: we are, and always will be, the United States of America.	**Carefully planned repetition can help to reinforce a message and also engage and rouse an audience so that they feel like they have participated in the speech; the sense of anticipation for the next repeated phrase helps to involve the audience.**
It's the answer that led those who have been told for so long by so many 1) **to be cynical, 2) and fearful, 3) and doubtful** of what we can achieve to put their hands on the arc of history and bend it once more toward the hope of a better day.	**Power of three**
It's been a long time coming, but tonight, **because of what we did on this day,** in this election, at this defining moment, change has come to America.	**Use of 'we' and 'you' creates the sense of a shared victory**

Chapter 5

VICTORY FOR THE PEOPLE

But above all, I will never forget who this victory truly belongs to - it belongs to you.

I was never the likeliest candidate for this office. We didn't start with much money or many endorsements. Our campaign was not hatched in the halls of Washington - it began in the backyards of Des Moines and the living rooms of Concord and the front porches of Charleston.

It was built by working men and women who dug into what little savings they had to give $5 and $10 and $20 to the cause.

It grew strength from the young people who rejected the myth of their generation's apathy; who left their homes and their families for jobs that offered little pay and less sleep; it grew strength from the not-so-young people who braved the bitter cold and scorching heat to knock on the doors of perfect strangers; from the millions of Americans who volunteered, and organised, and proved that more than two centuries later, a government of the people, by the people and for the people has not perished from the Earth.

This is your victory.

Providing stories of everyday people reinforces the idea that the triumph was one that all aspects of society contributed to.

THE TASK AHEAD

I know you didn't do this just to win an election and I know you didn't do it for me. You did it because you understand the enormity of the task that lies ahead. For even as we celebrate tonight, we know the challenges that tomorrow will bring are the greatest of our lifetime – 1) two wars, 2) a planet in peril, 3) the worst financial crisis in a century.

Even as we stand here tonight, we know there are brave Americans waking up in the deserts of Iraq and the mountains of Afghanistan to risk their lives for us.

There are mothers and fathers who will lie awake after their children fall asleep and wonder how they'll make the mortgage, or pay their doctor's bills, or save enough for their child's college education. There is new energy to harness and new jobs to be created; new schools to build and threats to meet and alliances to repair.

Depersonalises the victory – creates the impression he is a man of the people

Power of three

Showing empathy for those less fortunate
Power of three

Chapter 5

REMAKING THE NATION

The road ahead will be long. Our climb will be steep. We may not get there in one year or even in one term, but America - I have never been more hopeful than I am tonight that we will get there. I promise you - we as a people will get there.

There will be setbacks and false starts. There are many who won't agree with every decision or policy I make as president, and we know that government can't solve every problem. But I will always be honest with you about the challenges we face. I will listen to you, especially when we disagree.

And above all, I will ask you to join in the work of remaking this nation the only way it's been done in America for 221 years - block by block, brick by brick, calloused hand by calloused hand.

ONE NATION, ONE PEOPLE

What began 21 months ago in the depths of winter cannot end on this autumn night. This victory alone is not the change we seek - it is only the chance for us to make that change. And that cannot happen if we go back to the way things were. 1) It cannot happen without you, 2) without a new spirit of service, 3) a new spirit of sacrifice. So let us summon a new spirit of 1) patriotism; of 2) service and 3) responsibility where each of us resolves to pitch in and work harder and look after not only ourselves, but each other. Let us remember that if this financial crisis taught us anything, it's that we cannot have a thriving Wall Street while Main Street suffers - in this country, we rise or fall as one nation; as one people.

And to those Americans whose support I have yet to earn - I may not have won your vote tonight, 1) but I hear your voices, 2) I need your help, and 3) I will be your president too.

Use of metaphor to describe the journey ahead.

Effective use of dash to link ideas.

'we as a people' promotes the idea of a joint ownership and shared responsibility.

Use of short, simple sentence to produce more sombre, realistic mood (and expectation).

Effective use of the imagery of struggle.

Reveals that he is open to new ideas.

Power of three.

Use of adjective to act as a symbol of America's struggle to get to this point.

Use of alliteration to reinforce his plea to the nation & Power of three.

Chapter 5

AMERICA IN THE WORLD

To those who would tear the world down - we will defeat you. To those who seek peace and security - we support you.

And to all those who have wondered if America's beacon still burns as bright - tonight we proved once more that the true strength of our nation comes not from the might of our arms or the scale of our wealth, but from the enduring power of our ideals: democracy, liberty, opportunity and unyielding hope.

For that is the true genius of America - that America can change. Our union can be perfected. And what we have already achieved gives us hope for what we can and must achieve tomorrow.

A HISTORY OF STRUGGLE

This election had many firsts and many stories that will be told for generations. But one that's on my mind tonight is about a woman who cast her ballot in Atlanta. She's a lot like the millions of others who stood in line to make their voice heard in this election except for one thing - Ann Nixon Cooper is 106 years old.

She was born just a generation past slavery; a time when there were no cars on the road or planes in the sky; when someone like her couldn't vote for two reasons - because she was a woman and because of the colour of her skin.

And tonight, I think about all that she's seen throughout her century in America - the heartache and the hope; the struggle and the progress; the times we were told that we can't, and the people who pressed on with that American creed: *Yes, we can.*

At a time when women's voices were silenced and their hopes dismissed, she lived to see them stand up and speak out and reach for the ballot. *Yes, we can.*

When there was despair in the dust bowl and depression across the land, she saw a nation conquer fear itself with a New Deal, new jobs and a new sense of common purpose. *Yes, we can.*

Emotive abstract nouns create the feeling of unity and collective ownership

Acknowledgement of those who did not support him who he will still serve as President.

Displaying strong, resilient qualities in a bid to make people feel safe in the face of potential attacks.

Provides personal story of an 106 year old woman who has been through all the struggles and prejudices.

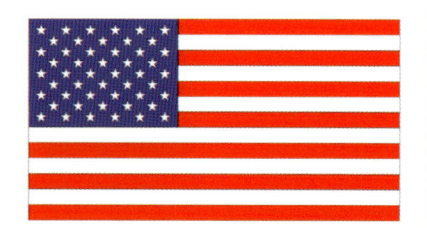

Chapter 5

When the bombs fell on our harbour and tyranny threatened the world, she was there to witness a generation rise to greatness and a democracy was saved. ==Yes, we can.==

She was there for the buses in Montgomery, the hoses in Birmingham, a bridge in Selma, and a preacher from Atlanta who told a people that "we shall overcome". ==Yes, we can.==

1) A man touched down on the Moon, 2) a wall came down in Berlin, 3) a world was connected by our own science and imagination. And this year, in this election, she touched her finger to a screen, and cast her vote, because after 106 years in America, through the best of times and the darkest of hours, she knows how America can change. ==Yes, we can.==

THIS IS OUR MOMENT

America, we have come so far. We have seen so much. But there is so much more to do. So tonight, let us ask ourselves - if our children should live to see the next century; if my daughters should be so lucky to live as long as Ann Nixon Cooper, what change will they see? What progress will we have made?

==This is our chance to answer that call. This is our moment.==

This is ==our== *time - to put our people back to work and open doors of opportunity for* ==our== *kids; to restore prosperity and promote the cause of peace; to reclaim the American dream and reaffirm that fundamental truth -* ==that out of many, we are one; that while we breathe, we hope, and where we are met with cynicism and doubt, and those who tell us that we can't, we will respond with that timeless creed that sums up the spirit of a people: yes, we can.==

Thank you, God bless you, and may God bless the United States of America.

As the speech nears its climax, the triumphant phrase 'Yes we can' is juxtaposed next to each achievement that is described; this helps to rally the crowd into a frenzy of hope, anticipation and expectancy.
Power of three.

Use of the word 'our' to reinforce message of working alongside each other - a shared dream and ownership.

Rhythm of speech helps to build up the climax.

Effective use of alliteration – 'spirit of the people'

How could I use these techniques in my own speech writing?

The amount of work that goes into a great speech, particular a President or Prime Minister, is enormous, with teams of people working extensively to find the right phrases to achieve the greatest effect on their audience.

Chapter 5 — **Challenge 9**

Finding your own voice

Choose a topic you feel strongly about, and practice using some of the techniques outlined in the previous pages. Read your lines to your learning partner and ask them how effective it was in convincing them of your views. You may wish to use:

- repetition for a particular effect
- personal stories to support your viewpoints
- power of 3
- metaphor to symbolise your points
- powerful adjectives/adverbs
- language that engages your audience in your viewpoint

You may wish to use some of the connective bank below to help express your ideas:

What has helped me learn effectively today?

Opinion and interpretation
it would seem
one might consider suggest
propose / deduce / infer
presumably
in the view of
on the strength of
to the best of one's belief
theoretically
literally
obviously
possibly
maybe
contrary to
improbably
incredibly

OBAMA
WWW.BARACKOBAMA.COM

Chapter 5 — Challenge 10

In pairs, read through the following speech and discuss where you believe the techniques listed below are used.

- Direct, informal appeal to the hearts of the public
- Creates the impression as a common man of the people
- Colloquial use of language. Dramatic use of short, powerful and brutally honest statement
- Use of 'us' which suggests that they are all in this situation together and must work as a team to recover
- Use of imagery/ emotional pleas/ Use of metaphorical journey
- Attaching on to a biblical reference as a device for sharing the public need for forgiveness
- Use of alliteration to suggest that he will be a better leader for the experience.
- Use of exaggerated adjectives / repetition for emphasise
- Variation in sentence length
- Extends rhetoric and use of powerful and personal stories, using the child in a way to symbolise the hopeful public reaction
- Use of repetition and religious references to suggest that if God will forgive them perhaps the public will also.
- Uses imagery of passage to symbolise his own situation
- Powerful and moving closing statement in which the President captures the theme of forgiveness in his final plea to the public.

In what other subjects could I apply these skills?

A President with a different purpose

Former President, Bill Clinton, delivered this speech after it had been revealed that he lied over an affair he had with a white house worker, Monica Lewinsky. Under severe pressure to resign, with his morality in question, Mr. Clinton tries desperately to win over the American people in order for them to forgive him for his lies.

Thank you very much, ladies and gentlemen. Welcome to the White House and to this day to which Hillary and the vice president and I look forward so much every year.
This is always an important day for our country, for the reasons that the vice president said.
It is an unusual and, I think, unusually important day today. I may not be quite as easy with my words today as I have been in years past, and I was up rather late last night thinking about and praying about what I ought to say today. And rather unusual for me, I actually tried to write it down.
So if you will forgive me, I will do my best to say what it is I want to say to you - and I may

Chapter 5

have to take my glasses out to read my own writing.

First, I want to say to all of you that, as you might imagine, I have been on quite a journey these last few weeks to get to the end of this, to the rock bottom truth of where I am and where we all are.

I agree with those who have said that in my first statement after I testified I was not contrite enough. I don't think there is a fancy way to say that I have sinned.

It is important to me that everybody who has been hurt know that the sorrow I feel is genuine: first and most important, my family; also my friends, my staff, my Cabinet, Monica Lewinsky and her family, and the American people. I have asked all for their forgiveness.

But I believe that to be forgiven, more than sorrow is required - at least two more things. First, genuine repentance - a determination to change and to repair breaches of my own making. I have repented. Second, what my bible calls a "broken spirit"; an understanding that I must have God's help to be the person that I want to be; a willingness to give the very forgiveness I seek; a renunciation of the pride and the anger which cloud judgment, lead people to excuse and compare and to blame and complain.

Now, what does all this mean for me and for us? First, I will instruct my lawyers to mount a vigorous defence, using all available appropriate arguments. But legal language must not obscure the fact that I have done wrong. Second, I will continue on the path of repentance, seeking pastoral support and that of other caring people so that they can hold me accountable for my own commitment.

Third, I will intensify my efforts to lead our country and the world toward peace and freedom, prosperity and harmony, in the hope that with a broken spirit and a still strong heart I can be used for greater good, for we have many blessings and many challenges and so much work to do.

In this, I ask for your prayers and for your help in healing our nation. And though I cannot move beyond or forget this - indeed, I must always keep it as a caution light in my life - it is very important that our nation move forward. I am very grateful for the many, many people - clergy and ordinary citizens alike - who have written me with wise counsel. I am profoundly grateful for the support of so many Americans who somehow through it all seem to still know that I care about them a great deal, that I care about their problems and their dreams. I am grateful for those who have stood by me and who say that in this case and many others, the bounds of privacy have been excessively and unwisely invaded. That may be. Nevertheless, in this case, it may be a blessing, because I still sinned. And if my repentance is genuine and sustained, and if I can maintain both a broken spirit and a strong heart, then good can come of this for our country as well as for me and my family.

The children of this country can learn in a profound way that integrity is important and selfishness is wrong, but God can change us and make us strong at the broken places. I want to embody those lessons for the children of this country - for that little boy in Florida who came up to me and said that he wanted to grow up and be President and to be just like me. I want the parents of all the children in America to be able to say that to their children. A couple of days ago when I was in Florida a Jewish friend of mine gave me this liturgy book called "Gates of Repentance." And there was this incredible passage from the Yom Kippur liturgy. I would like to read it to you: "Now is the time for turning. The leaves are beginning to turn from green to red to orange.

Chapter 5

The birds are beginning to turn and are heading once more toward the south. The animals are beginning to turn to storing their food for the winter. For leaves, birds and animals, turning comes instinctively. But for us, turning does not come so easily. It takes an act of will for us to make a turn. It means breaking old habits. It means admitting that we have been wrong, and this is never easy. It means losing face.

In this, I ask for your prayers and for your help in healing our nation. And though I cannot move beyond or forget this - indeed, I must always keep it as a caution light in my life - it is very important that our nation move forward. I am very grateful for the many, many people - clergy and ordinary citizens alike - who have written me with wise counsel. I am profoundly grateful for the support of so many Americans who somehow through it all seem to still know that I care about them a great deal, that I care about their problems and their dreams. I am grateful for those who have stood by me and who say that in this case and many others, the bounds of privacy have been excessively and unwisely invaded. That may be. Nevertheless, in this case, it may be a blessing, because I still sinned. And if my repentance is genuine and sustained, and if I can maintain both a broken spirit and a strong heart, then good can come of this for our country as well as for me and my family.

The children of this country can learn in a profound way that integrity is important and selfishness is wrong, but God can change us and make us strong at the broken places. I want to embody those lessons for the children of this country - for that little boy in Florida who came up to me and said that he wanted to grow up and be President and to be just like me. I want the parents of all the children in America to be able to say that to their children.

A couple of days ago when I was in Florida a Jewish friend of mine gave me this liturgy book called "Gates of Repentance." And there was this incredible passage from the Yom Kippur liturgy. I would like to read it to you:
It means starting all over again. And this is always painful. It means saying I am sorry. It means recognizing that we have the ability to change. These things are terribly hard to do. But unless we turn, we will be trapped forever in yesterday's ways. Lord help us to turn, from callousness to sensitivity, from hostility to love, from pettiness to purpose, from envy to contentment, from carelessness to discipline, from fear to faith. Turn us around, O Lord, and bring us back toward you. Revive our lives as at the beginning, and turn us toward each other, Lord, for in isolation there is no life."

I thank my friend for that. I thank you for being here. I ask you to share my prayer that God will search me and know my heart, try me and know my anxious thoughts, see if there is any hurtfulness in me, and lead me toward the life everlasting. I ask that God give me a clean heart, let me walk by faith and not sight.

I ask once again to be able to love my neighbour - all my neighbours - as my self, to be an instrument of God's peace; to let the words of my mouth and the meditations of my heart and, in the end, the work of my hands, be pleasing. This is what I wanted to say to you today.

Thank you. God bless you.
President Bill Clinton

Chapter 5

What makes this an effective and convincing speech?

Firstly we need to consider the following:

What is the former President's purpose?

1. To apologise to the American public about the scandal
2. To regain the public confidence in his ability as a leader.
3. To attempt to put the situation behind him.

What tone/style should it be in?

Compassionate/ Sensitive
Apologetic / Remorseful
Repentant / Strong /Assertive
Showing that he is able to learn from mistakes

Challenge 11

Comment on detail on whether you believe that Bill Clinton was successful in achieving his purpose. Consider the prompts below.

Use examples to justify your views.

- direct appeal to the listener
- use of alliteration
- use of imagery and metaphorical language
- using a personal story
- rhetorical questions
- short, direct statements
- repetition
- joining the public with himself.
- exaggeration
- use of powerful adjectives
- use of emotive language

As you can see there are many devices needed to make a great and convincing speech.

Chapter 5

Challenge 12

Think of an occasion where you might need to change someone's opinions – it could be because they have stereotypical views or because they support a team you don't like too much!

Produce a persuasive speech in which you try out some of the techniques that you have already examined. You may wish to use some of the connectives in the table to help link your ideas:

Persuasion
of course
naturally
obviously
clearly
evidently
surely
certainly
decidedly
indeed
virtually
no wonder
strangely enough
oddly enough
luckily
(un)fortunately
admittedly
undoubtedly

Handling emotions effectively

The following speech was delivered at the funeral of Princess Diana by her brother, Earl Charles Spencer. Princess Diana was killed in a road accident in Paris, whilst being chased by the Paparazzi (photographers who follow the famous)

It is clear that the aims of this speech were to:

- pay tribute to the memory of his sister
- vent his anger and disgust at the way his sister was treated by others, particularly the media
- reveal his feelings towards the royal family
- communicate his fears for the future of Prince William and Prince Harry

When could I use these skills outside of school?

Chapter 5 — Challenge 13

As you read through this speech, consider how this anger and deep emotion is controlled to have the most impact on the public. In groups of 4, pick out examples of the points made above and comment on the language used. Some examples have been highlighted for you.

I stand before you today the representative of a family in grief, in a country in mourning before a world in shock. We are all united not only in our desire to pay our respects to Diana but rather in our need to do so. For such was her ==extraordinary appeal== that the tens of millions of people taking part in this service all over the world via television and radio who never actually met her, feel that they too lost someone close to them in the early hours of Sunday morning. It is a more remarkable tribute to Diana than I can ever hope to offer her today.

Diana was the ==very essence of compassion, of duty, of style, of beauty==. All over the world she was a symbol of selfless humanity. All over the world, a standard bearer for the rights of the truly downtrodden, a very British girl who transcended nationality. Someone with a ==natural nobility== who was classless and who proved in the last year that she needed no royal title to continue to generate her particular brand of magic.

Today is our chance to say thank you for the way ==you brightened our lives,== even though God granted you but half a life. We will all feel cheated always that you were taken from us so young and yet ==we must learn to be grateful that you came along at all==. Only now that you are gone do we truly appreciate what we are now without and we want you to know that life without you is very, very difficult.

We have all despaired at our loss over the past week and only the strength of the message you gave us through your years of giving has afforded us the strength to move forward.

There is a temptation to rush to canonise your memory, there is no need to do so. You stand tall enough as a human being of unique qualities not to need to be seen as a saint. Indeed to sanctify your memory would be to miss out on the very core of your being, your wonderfully mischievous sense of humour with a laugh that bent you double.

==Your joy for life transmitted where ever you took your smile and the sparkle in those unforgettable eyes. Your boundless energy which you could barely contain.==

But your greatest gift was your intuition and it was a gift you used wisely. This is what underpinned all your other wonderful attributes and if we look to analyse what it was about you that had such a wide appeal we find it in your instinctive feel for what was really important in all our lives.

==Without your God-given sensitivity== we would be immersed in greater ignorance at the anguish of Aids and HIV sufferers, the plight of the homeless, the isolation of lepers, the random destruction of landmines.

Diana explained to me once that it was her innermost feelings of suffering that made it possible for her to connect with her constituency of the rejected.

And here we come to another truth about her. For all the status, the glamour, the applause, Diana remained throughout a very insecure person at heart, almost childlike in her desire to do good for others so she could release herself from deep feelings of unworthiness of which her eating disorders were merely a symptom.

The world sensed this part of her character and ==cherished her for her vulnerability whilst admiring her for her honesty.==

What has helped me learn effectively today?

Chapter 5

The last time I saw Diana was on July 1, her birthday in London, when typically she was not taking time to celebrate her special day with friends but was guest of honour at a special charity fundraising evening. She sparkled of course, but I would rather cherish the days I spent with her in March when she came to visit me and my children in our home in South Africa. I am proud of the fact apart from when she was on display meeting President Mandela we managed to contrive to stop the ever-present paparazzi from getting a single picture of her - that meant a lot to her.

These were days I will always treasure. It was as if we had been transported back to our childhood when we spent such an enormous amount of time together - the two youngest in the family.

Fundamentally she had not changed at all from the big sister who mothered me as a baby, fought with me at school and endured those long train journeys between our parents' homes with me at weekends.

It is a tribute to her level-headedness and strength that despite the most bizarre-like life imaginable after her childhood, she remained intact, true to herself.

There is no doubt that she was looking for a new direction in her life at this time. She talked endlessly of getting away from England, mainly because of the treatment that she received at the hands of the newspapers. I don't think she ever understood why her genuinely good intentions were sneered at by the media, why there appeared to be a permanent quest on their behalf to bring her down. It is baffling.

My own and only explanation is that genuine goodness is threatening to those at the opposite end of the moral spectrum. It is a point to remember that of all the ironies about Diana, perhaps the greatest was this - a girl given the name of the ancient goddess of hunting was, in the end, the most hunted person of the modern age.

She would want us today to pledge ourselves to protecting her beloved boys William and Harry from a similar fate and I do this here Diana on your behalf. We will not allow them to suffer the anguish that used regularly to drive you to tearful despair.

And beyond that, on behalf of your mother and sisters, I pledge that we, your blood family, will do all we can to continue the imaginative way in which you were steering these two exceptional young men so that their souls are not simply immersed by duty and tradition but can sing openly as you planned.

We fully respect the heritage into which they have both been born and will always respect and encourage them in their royal role but we, like you, recognise the need for them to experience as many different aspects of life as possible to arm them spiritually and emotionally for the years ahead. I know you would have expected nothing less from us.

William and Harry, we all cared desperately for you today. We are all chewed up with the sadness at the loss of a woman who was not even our mother. How great your suffering is, we cannot even imagine.

I would like to end by thanking God for the small mercies he has shown us at this dreadful time. For taking Diana at her most beautiful and radiant and when she had joy in her private life. Above all we give thanks for the life of a woman I am so proud to be able to call my sister, the unique, the complex, the extraordinary and irreplaceable Diana whose beauty, both internal and external, will never be extinguished from our minds.

Chapter 5

How does Earl Charles Spencer communicate his own 'voice' through using literary devices?

As well as the way that Princess Diana was described, in what she achieved, and what she stood for, Charles Spencer also uses subtlety when discussing the royal family's involvement in her demise.

For example, when he says that his sister was.

Someone with a natural nobility who was classless and who proved in the last year that she needed no royal title to continue to generate her particular brand of magic.

This is a subtle criticism of the hierarchy and snobbery of the royal family who were a hindrance to Diana's work; in particular, the rather dismissive phrase 'needed no royal title' reinforces the idea that Diana was cherished in spite of her royal status, rather than because of it.

Earl Charles Spencer also remarks that.

We fully respect the heritage into which they have both been born and will always respect and encourage them in their royal role

He is acknowledging and respecting the public's view on the royal family whilst using the simple connective and following statement:

but we, like you, recognise the need for them to experience as many different aspects of life as possible to arm them spiritually and emotionally for the years ahead.

His use of the phrase 'but we, like you' engages and involves the public in his point of view, which creates the impression that it is a shared view that the Princes', unlike Diana, should be allowed to experience life outside the royal family, without the fear of being excluded.

When he comments that Diana was taken **"at her most beautiful and radiant and when she had joy in her private life"** suggests that her public and personal life whilst a member of the royal family (when married to Prince Charles) was one of unhappiness.

Applying these skills:
Practice making a statement about something you feel angry and upset about without being too obvious - use subtlety.

Chapter 5

Challenge 14

Look at the following descriptions of Diana, and use the same techniques to describe someone who is close to you.

Technique	Diana speech	Your own speech
Description of appearance and personality	extraordinary appeal very essence of compassion, of duty, of style, of beauty natural nobility God-given sensitivity But your greatest gift was your intuition and it was a gift you used wisely	
Explanation of what has been achieved. The way that people have been affected	All over the world she was a symbol of selfless humanity. All over the world, a standard bearer for the rights of the truly downtrodden,	

Challenge 15

Using the ideas above, you need to write a detailed speech with the titles below. Remember to be assertive not aggressive. Confident, not arrogant. Convincing not threatening!

Homelessness
The treatment of homeless people is nothing short of a disgrace.

Smoking
Whether smoking should be banned altogether should really not be up for debate in view of the thousands of lives it takes every day.

Euthanasia
Putting a grieving relative in prison for easing the terrible pain of their loved one is an unforgivable part of our so called justice system.

Crime
It is possible to reduce the chances of crime if we only took greater care of ourselves.

Chapter 5

Developing viewpoint and voice through commentary

A commentary could be described as voicing an opinion on something which you feel strongly about; this does not necessarily involve an emotive issue, and could describe someone's excitement or despair about a TV programme or new PS3 game.

Some techniques of writing an effective commentary could be to

Use humour in your writing through sarcasm and irony:	*Of course teenagers love to wear the cardboard shirts, the old fashioned blazers, and those, oh so nice, awkward fitting trousers. Who in their right mind would want to wear their own, more comfortable clothes to school when sitting behind a desk all day.*
You may wish to use exaggeration	*There he was with that massive red boil on his nose as the unripened tomatoes looked on in envy.*
You may wish to interact with your reader, using rhetorical questions	*I don't care if people don't like playing dominoes – I'm not asking them to. Do I come into your house and say 'Stop doing what you enjoy because it's boring'.*

Commenting effectively on an emotive issue

When you feel strongly about an issue, it is very easy to communicate your thoughts, either through speech or in writing in an overly emotional way which lacks focus and direction, therefore running the risk of coming across simply as angry, rather than assertive in tone. In the following article, the case against legalising Euthanasia (the act of painless killing to remove suffering) is put forward to the public. Consider how effectively this has been presented to the reader through the use of factual evidence rather than an overly emotive response.

Chapter 5

Non-Religious Arguments against 'Voluntary Euthanasia'

1. Legalising the deliberate killing of humans (other than in legitimate self-defence/war or possibly for the most heinous of crimes) fundamentally undermines the basis of law and public morality.
2. No system of safeguards could ever be foolproof, so in practice legalising 'voluntary euthanasia' would result in legalising involuntary euthanasia. This has been the experience in both Nazi Germany and, currently, in Holland.(ref)
3. Legalising 'voluntary euthanasia' on the basis of excruciating 'hard cases' would result in its being routinely practiced on a large scale. Bad cases do not make good law. One leading medical ethicist said more than twenty years ago "We shall begin by doing it because the patient is in intolerable pain but we shall end up doing it because it is Friday afternoon and we want to get away for the weekend"[1]. The precedent of abortion is chilling: "Aging Advisory Services" would offer a 1-stop shop where you could pop in your inconvenient relatives and, for a suitable fee, euthanasia them in your lunch-hour.
4. Even if someone sincerely wants to be euthanasia this may well be due to depression or to a misapprehension of their true prognosis. Palliative specialists report that such requests are often used by patients to assess their worth and value to others. A positive response merely confirms their worst fears and such a decision, once acted upon, is irreversible.
5. Legalised euthanasia would produce huge social pressures on very vulnerable people to 'volunteer', causing much stress and suffering.
6. It would undermine the financing and provision of proper geriatric and palliative care: with stretched budgets euthanasia would be see as the cost-effective option. Indeed it would be very "cost effective".
7. It would also undermine funding of research into these areas.
8. Even without it being explicitly stated, legalising euthanasia (and presumably making it available on the NHS) would mean that the state was offering it as an alternative to people who were seeking benefits for sickness or unemployment or to pensioners, to refugees and people with disabilities. If it were legalised, why not then insist that such people have 'euthanasia counselling' before they receive care or benefits?
9. It would fundamentally undermine the relationships between elderly or dependent relatives and their families, with overwhelming pressures being applied on people to 'take the honourable course' and 'not be a burden'.
10. It would fundamentally undermine the basis of trust between doctors and patients that is at the heart of effective medicine. Many people in Holland are rightly terrified of going to hospital and being euthanised against their will. Far from being the 'ultimate expression of patient autonomy' legalised euthanasia becomes the ultimate act of medical paternalism.
11. Any form of suicide is devastating for the people left behind who love the person who has decided that his or her life is no longer worth living: it is especially damaging for children.
12. Whereas the advocates of euthanasia are mostly members of the chattering classes who seem to be having difficulty in coming to terms with their own mortality, the victims would predominantly be the most disadvantaged members of society: the old, poor, disabled, infirm and unemployed.
13. Euthanasia would be executed by people who think "I have a much higher IQ and am much better educated than most of the people" with whom they interact, and claim to "know with complete certainty" that the deepest beliefs and aspirations of others are groundless.

Chapter 5 — Challenge 16

What techniques could I use in writing my own commentary?
It is important to consider the persuasive techniques used by the writers as well as how convincing their argument comes across the reader. Pick out examples of these persuasive techniques. Some have been done for you.

Immediate use of the words 'Non religious' which would avoid people wrongly judging this argument as a religious one

Use of numbered points helps to create the factual tone, therefore creating the sense it is objective and authentic (unbiased, real and true)

Use of supporting evidence

Short, dramatic statement used to good effect

Use of research to back up points

Non-Religious Arguments against 'Voluntary Euthanasia'
by Nicholas Beale and Prof. Stuart Horner MD
(former Chairman, BMA Medical Ethics Committee)

1. Legalising the deliberate killing of humans (other than in legitimate self-defence/war or possibly for the most heinous of crimes) fundamentally undermines the basis of law and public morality.
2. No system of safeguards could ever be foolproof, so in practice legalising 'voluntary euthanasia' would result in legalising involuntary euthanasia. This has been the experience in both Nazi Germany and, currently, in Holland.
3. Legalising 'voluntary euthanasia' on the basis of excruciating 'hard cases' would result in its being routinely practiced on a large scale. Bad cases do not make good law. One leading medical ethicist said more than twenty years ago "We shall begin by doing it because the patient is in intolerable pain but we shall end up doing it because it is Friday afternoon and we want to get away for the weekend"[1]. The precedent of abortion is chilling: "Aging Advisory Services" would offer a 1-stop shop where you could pop in your inconvenient relatives and, for a suitable fee, euthanase them in your lunch-hour.
4. Even if someone sincerely wants to use euthanasia, this may well be due to depression or to a misapprehension of their true prognosis. Palliative specialists report that such requests are often used by patients to assess their worth and value to others. A positive response merely confirms their worst fears and such a decision, once acted upon, is irreversible.
5. Legalised euthanasia would produce huge social pressures on very vulnerable people to 'volunteer', causing much stress and suffering.
6. It would undermine the financing and provision of proper geriatric and palliative care: with stretched budgets euthanasia would be see as the cost-effective option. Indeed it would be very "cost effective".

Chapter 5

Writing a commentary

The following article is a commentary on the Hollywood film industry, and in particular the thriller genre which can often be shown to be extremely formulaic (predictable with an over used plot)

Challenge 17

Read through this article and consider how the writer uses humour to criticise the lack of originality in films that are being produced today.

Pick out the phrases that demonstrate that this writer is mocking (taking the mickey!) the film industry. You need to decide on what these words and phrases reveal about the writer's thoughts on the film industry.

Familiarity breeds contempt – films that have lost the plot.

Former detective/ FBI agent/army officer begins his retirement from work yet there is just one more case that he can't resist. His former employees are very insistent, and eventually drag him from retirement. He will probably be chopping logs on a deserted cabin.

He aggress. Perhaps its because he is personally involved as a family member who has been caught up with it all. When returning back to work, he usually has to work with a young up-start who has new ways of working and they clash regularly. At one point the former detective/FBI agent/army officer goes too far because of his old unorthodox methods of working and there is a scene where is boss tells him he has been taken off the case. This leads to a dramatic scene where he is forced to hand over his gun and then his badge. However he has not given up and seeks contact with his secret friends in the organisation who risk there own job by finding out important information. This involving lots of computer screens, dusty filing cabinets and messages saying RESTRICTED ACCESS UNLOCK CODE ACCESS DENIED DELETE FILES (ARE YOU SURE YOU WISH TO DELETE FILES)etc. etc. He even develops an unlikely bond with the younger, less experienced, more cautious and rigid colleague. He will meet some woman along the way who is attracted and perplexed in equal measure by his rebellious yet effective ways. She will probably help him with the case. The baddie will toy with him, sending him messages and playing mind games with him. There will probably be a scene where he almost catches him, runs through a busy street and gets the guy in the black overcoat, only to realise his only crime is wearing the exactly same black coat as the criminal. All of this eventually leads him to catch the baddy. He is usually a serial killer who has a personal vendetta with our hero. He has a climatic battle with the baddie, usually on a roof, or boat, or disused factory, car park (often involving lifts and smashing through levels of glass). At one point it looks as if evil with triumph, but just as our hero is about to fall of that huge tower block, an unlikely source comes to his rescue (this can either be the love interest, the young-upstart or a former colleague who has been against our hero for the whole film yet now decides to rescue him) Good triumphs over evil by the end and his former employees have a joke and a knowing look towards their hero – in spite of his mischievous working practice. Seems familiar? You are probably wondering why you have sat through so many of these films which have an identical plot and characters – the only difference is that the actors are different, well sometimes!

Chapter 5

Developing opinions on a topical issue.

Soap Operas, or Soaps as they're commonly known, have a huge impact on today's society – not just because of their high ratings and popularity, but because their appeal is so wide and far reaching. Read through the commentary below which discusses the various reasons why soaps may be so popular.

Why are soaps so popular?

There can be little doubt that the success of soaps is largely down to the audience being able to identify with the characters – however extreme and unrealistic there actions can be at times. We feel sympathy, hate and admiration towards some of the characters (victims/villain/heroes).

Moreover they are educational as well as having a positive impact – there has been evidence of a huge increase of phone calls to care lines if a popular soap has raised the issue. Soaps also give moral guidance and show the effects and consequences of choosing wrong from right. It could also be argued that they help people to escape from their own lives.

Typical Features of the Soap Opera

Setting.
Must be a communal places where people are likely to meet. Work places will generally offer a service to the public (the other characters) Examples include pubs, garages, shops, markets cafes, laundrettes etc.

Plot and narrative setting.
Individual episodes will often reflect a common theme or mood. Beginning of each episode usually involves reminders to the audience of the past episode – allowing the feeling of ownership of the programme and security that you can catch up if you may have missed an episode. Cliff hangers are used frequently and there is rarely closure. Scenes are juxtaposed (placed together) for dramatic effect often or to help reinforce the theme of the episode.

Characterisation.
Stereotypes are often used. For example, the victim, hardman, prankster, gossip, peacemaker) Soaps are often criticised for reinforcing national stereotypes.

For example, the drunken, aggressive Scottish/Irish Man – Jim from Coronation Street or Trevor from Eastenders. Other examples include the Asian corner shop, the wide boy market trader or local East end gangster. Relationships and marriages rarely last, with the emphasis usually being on the man being unfaithful. Also, there are a high turnover of characters and consequently 'deaths' Ian Beale from EastEnders has had three wives so far – two have died tragically (Cindy and Laura) and one has divorced him and gone for good. (Melanie)

Themes and Issues.
General themes include topics such as class, race, gender relationships, morality. Or more specific emotive issues such as euthanasia, bereavement, domestic violence, AIDS, homelessness, bullying etc.

Chapter 5

Challenge 18

Using this article and your own knowledge of soaps (try not to do too much research or you'll have no time for homework!) complete the 3 tasks below. Remember to include details of the main language and presentational features of this type of writing.

1	Analyse	The reasons why soaps are so popular in British culture. Consider the reasons given above and provide a personal response to these, using your own analysis of soaps.
2	Review	a soap of your choice. You will need to discuss how effectively the soap manages to: • Be realistic • Have interesting storylines • Produce characters you can relate to • Deal with issues in a sensitive and thought provoking way.
3	Comment	On whether soaps are overrated and bad for teenagers or do they have a important role in a teenager's life.

You may wish to use some of the phrases in the connective bank on the next page to support your ideas:

Chapter 5

Using connectives to discuss a topical issue

Opinion and interpretation	Contrast and balance	Illustration
it would seem	but	for example
one might consider suggest	however	for instance
propose/deduce/infer	nevertheless	such as
presumably	alternatively	as
in the view of	to turn to	as revealed by
on the strength of	yet	thus
to the best of one's belief	despite this	to show that
theoretically	on the contrary	to take the case of
literally	as for	to elucidate
obviously	the opposite	that is to say
possibly	still	in other words
maybe	instead	a case in point
contrary to	on the other hand	an instance
improbably	whereas	
incredibly	otherwise	
	although	
	apart from	
	equally	
	to balance this	
	all the same	
	for all that	
	albeit/though	
	taking one thing with another	
	it is dou	
	confuting this/disputing this	

Chapter 5

Using role models to explore a topic.

The following two extracts are good examples of how positive role models who are in the public eye can communicate a message effectively.

In the first one, Rio Ferdinand (Manchester United and England footballer) discusses his views and experiences of racism.

RIO FERDINAND: Football is a great way to defeat the racists

By Damien Fletcher 30/04/2008

The latest England football captain Rio Ferdinand personally experienced racism but refused to suffer in silence. Here he speaks about how he dealt with it – and how you can follow his example…

I grew up in Peckham, South London, which is a multicultural area. Every now and again there was the odd bit of racism but I was lucky, it was very limited.

The place where I experienced it more often was at football, which was weird. I played in a predominantly white area away from where I grew up and I did have to deal with racism there.

The first thing I did was tell my coach which was important. Kids should always do that. Don't be scared and think, 'I'm a grass' or something like that.

When it comes to racism or being bullied the person in charge, the nearest adult is the first person to tell so they can nip it in the bud straight away.

The racist never came back so that was a good result – and we won the match on the day.

There are ways to combat racism and telling a responsible adult should always be the first thing you do.

I experienced it watching matches in the stands as well. I was about 13 and my friend managed to get some tickets and we were sitting enjoying the game.

There were some black players on the away team and the guy in front was shouting racist comments like, "go back to where you're from" and making noises. I was just thinking, "what's going on?"

There was a policeman standing two yards away, so I looked at him expecting some action and he looked right through me and carried on watching the game.

I thought to myself, 'he can hear it, I can hear it, so what's he going to do?'. Then I thought the man would stop, but something happened on the pitch and he started again.

Then after all the things he'd said, he turned to me and said, 'You're all right mate, it's just them ones on the pitch.' I looked at the policeman, shook my head and left.

Chapter 5

My advice to young people being racially abused is don't react if possible. Of course you can really feel like retaliating in some way, but I'd advise everyone to steer away from that because you come down to their level.

Tell an adult, a teacher, anyone who's responsible and can deal with the situation because you don't want to be starting fights and stuff like that, you'll become part of the problem.

Hopefully when the person gets dealt with the other children who've seen what happened won't go down that same route because they'll have seen that you get treated harshly by the teachers.

English football is leading the way in our response to racism and we've got to make sure that we keep going because we want other countries to follow our example.

In some places, Spain and certain Eastern Bloc countries come to mind, they perhaps don't see as many black people as we do because it's not as multicultural as the UK and that can create problems.

Obviously, racism goes beyond football and affects the whole society, but football is a great tool to combat racism and it needs to be used a lot more.

Punishments for racist behaviour need to be stepped up around the world. There needs to be serious.

Challenge 19

1) As a teenager, how does this article appeal to you?
2) How would this have had a different impact if it was someone you did not know?

Challenge 20

In the next article journalist, Tim Walker, discusses the appeal of Jay Z. As with the previous article, consider how, you as a teenager, may be inspired by this commentary of Jay Z's life and work to date.

Chapter 5

THE INDEPENDENT
By Tim Walker Saturday, 12 April 2008

JAY-Z: THE HUSTLER
HE'S THE GREATEST RAPPER ALIVE.

Jay-Z appeals to people who don't necessarily get hip-hop

A Life in Brief

Born Brooklyn, New York, 4 December 1969.
Family became involved with his partner Beyoncé Knowles after working together in 2002; rumoured to have married last week.
Education Dropped out of George Westinghouse Information Technology High School, Brooklyn, also the former school of Busta Rhymes and The Notorious B.I.G.
Career Ten solo albums including Reasonable Doubt (1996), Hard Knock Life (1998), The Blueprint (2001), The Black Album (2003). Was CEO of hip-hop record labels Def Jam and Roc-A-Fella.
He says "I was forced to be an artist and a CEO from the beginning. I was forced to be like a businessman because when I was trying to get a record deal, it was so hard to get a record deal on my own that it was either give up or create my own company."
They say "I think he's a genius." – Chris Martin of Coldplay.
Jay-Z gave Barack Obama advice on winning the hearts and minds of America's hip-hop community

---

Kanye might have the charisma; Fiddy might have the bullet wounds, and Diddy might have the overpriced perfume with his name all over it. But the rapper with the $150m deal is Jay-Z.

While the UK music press argues about his place on the Glastonbury line-up, Jay-Z can relax and count his blessings. Last week, he became the first hip-hop artist to sign a "360-degree" deal with concert promoters Live Nation, giving them a stake in all his myriad enterprises, and adding considerably to his personal fortune, already estimated at more than half a billion dollars.

The sum of $150m is more substantial than the price tag the promoter placed on Madonna ($120m) or U2 (a rumoured $100m-plus), and will see Live Nation funding not only Jay-Z's live performances, but also his next three albums to the tune of $10m each. The company will even pump $25m into his other business ventures, including clothing lines and a talent-spotting agency.

Chapter 5

According to reports, Jay-Z also took time off last weekend to marry Beyoncé Knowles. Yet somehow even a relationship conducted under the noses of the hungry US tabloids has failed to dent his critical standing. After more than a decade of remarkable commercial success, Jay-Z remains beloved of hardcore hip-hop fans and mere hobbyists alike.

"He's the greatest rapper alive," says Trevor Nelson, the hip-hop DJ and presenter. "The most credible rappers, like Common, never tend to be multi-platinum artists. The most commercial rappers, like 50 Cent, never get into the hall of fame for their skills. But Jay-Z has both, and that's what makes him great."

Jay-Z was born Shawn Corey Carter in Brooklyn in 1969. His mother Gloria recalls her son's birth on a recording made for "December 4th", a track from 2003's The Black Album: "Sean Carter was born December 4th/ weighing in at 10 pounds eight ounces/ He was the last of my four children/ The only one who didn't give me any pain when I gave birth to him/ and that's how I knew he was a special child."

Carter grew up in the Marcy Houses project in Bedford-Stuyvesant, in the shadow of the Brooklyn Bridge, close to the subway station on Marcy Avenue where the J and Z trains both stop. Marcy Houses' 4,000-plus residents are squeezed into 1,700 apartments in 27 six-storey buildings; the housing project was built in 1949, and by the time of Carter's birth it was one of the city's roughest neighbourhoods.

Carter's father left home when he was 12 years old, and he was raised by his mother, to whom he remains very close. She recalls on "December 4th" that the young Shawn would keep his three elder siblings awake at night, drumming the kitchen table and rapping. Eventually, she bought him a boom-box for his birthday, and he began making his own rhymes. Such are his self-taught skills that Jay-Z supposedly never writes his lyrics down on paper, and The Blueprint, one of his most critically and commercially popular albums, was written in just two days.

Jay-Z has always been ready to collaborate with artists from other genres, and that, too, displays his shrewd business sense. One of his most popular tracks is the mash-up "Numb/Encore" with his rapping layered over the crunching guitars of a Linkin Park song. On one of Jay-Z's most recent visits to the UK, Chris Martin of Coldplay joined him on stage at the Royal Albert Hall. And, most famously of all, he produced and performed on Beyoncé's breakout solo hit "Crazy in Love".

"The first time I met Chris Martin, he said 'I'm such a big fan of Jay-Z,'" Nelson recalls, "and I thought he's probably just saying that. But a year later they collaborated. Jay-Z appeals to people who don't necessarily get hip-hop."

That mainstream legitimacy has allowed Jay-Z access to a world beyond the imaginations of many of his Brooklyn contemporaries. Earlier this year, for example, he and Kanye West were consulted by Barack "B-Rock" Obama for their advice on winning the hearts and minds of America's hip-hop community. Trevor Nelson introduced Jay-Z to Prince Charles at a Prince's Trust event in 2004. "They had a little word about Beyoncé, and giggled about William being a fan. You could sense Jay-Z

But one thing is certain. If Jay-Z were really so wary of appearing, he wouldn't have agreed to it in the first place. He has always walked the tightrope between critical adoration and commercial success with enviable poise. Now, paradoxically, his fortune allows him to keep it just as real as ever. "The great thing for me is that I don't have to do anything for the money," he said recently. "I only do it because I like it."

Chapter 5 **Chapter 21**

Writing a review

In threes, take on the following roles:
a) Recorder (listens and make notes)
b) For
c) Against

1) Firstly choose something that you have all read/seen/played
2) Decide who will be A, B and C.
3) Discuss your choice for exactly 60 seconds whilst the recorder fills in a table such as the one below:

Book/Film/Game:	
For	Against

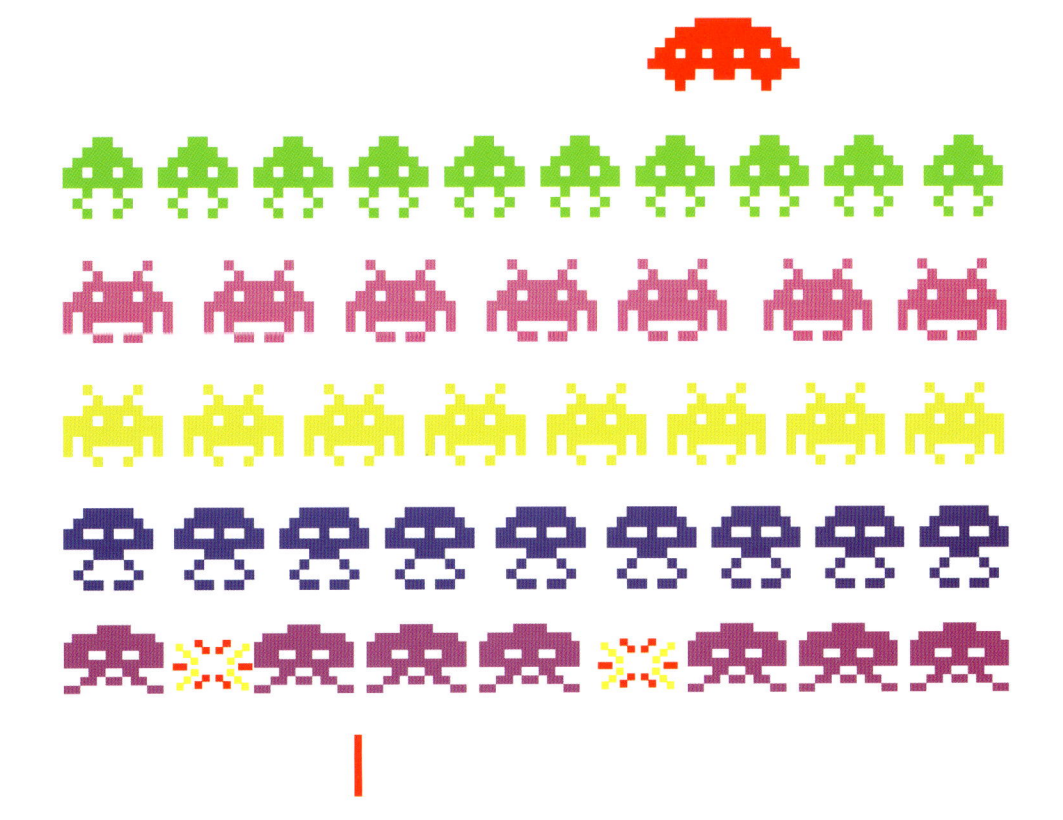

In your three, discuss how you could use sub-headings for the way the discussion took place. For example, if reviewing a game it could be:

- Graphics
- Playability
- Price

Chapter 5 — Challenge 22

In this article, there is a review of the PS3 and Wii. In pairs, you need to play the role of an editor in terms of cutting and reshaping this article so it is more appealing for a teenage audience.

Which video game console is better: PlayStation 3 or Wii?

Results so far:

PS3	39%	276 VOTES	TOTAL 709 VOTES
Wii	61%	433 VOTES	

by Sam Yang

It seems like people these days do not read nor do they pay close attention to the products that are advertised today. This is a perfect example of a simple question made complicated. PS3 and the Wii - which is the better console of the two?

This is not a hard question to answer nor is it a difficult one. I personally own a PS3 and a Wii. And let's get it straighten out once and for all. Hands down the PS3 is a superior machine than the Wii. We do not need to go into the details about the tech specs. Let us just compare the two consoles with simple comparisons shall we?

First up the Wii - Does not support high definition resolutions. Sure it has 480p but with 720p and 1080p out right now, why do you want to get the lowest of the 3?
Wii's remote controller does not support rechargeable batteries. You actually have to purchase batteries or rechargeable batteries for your Wii. Therefore, you'll be spending extra dollars every week, like me.
Video play back. The Wii does not support any video playback. The sad thing is that it is using a DVD drive which has the compatibilities of playings DVD movies but doesn't. Though this is just a gaming console, with the technology these days it is common sense to have a DVD player on your gaming console.

The Wii has 3 different controllers for consumers to purchase. For some games you will need to purchase 2 of the 3 different controllers in order to play certain games. That is a drawback because, again, you are spending more money on controllers than the actual games itself. The Wii does not support next-gen graphics. This is suppose to be a next-gen console correct? So then where is the graphics? The games being released on the Wii is looking like XBOX games.

That's not saying a lot which what the technology has to offer these days. Some developers such as Sega have already downloaded the Wii system. A gimmick - it's the controller that is worth 250.00 and not the overall console.

Chapter 5

And now for the PS3 - With the recent price drop of the PS3 being at 499.99 with 5 blu ray dvds, that is a tough, tough, bargain not to take. Blu Ray movies are at least 24.99 each and to get 5 of them for free? It's a no brainer for those that want to see what high definition looks like.

Availability. Even with the PS3 selling better than before, you are still able to find it at stores. Where is the Wii? Nintendo is controlling the market and the demands for the systems in which they can sell them at a higher price to stores for more money. A cheap, dirty way, if you ask me.

Next generation graphics. With the PS3 that is what you get. 499.99 isn't cheap and it sure doesn't give you have cheap hardware and technologies either. You have games with outputs in 720p and 1080p. What does that mean? The best resolution in today's market. Your eyes will love what it sees.

The games. People say the PS3 doesn't have the games to back up such a powerful system like the XBOX 360. Give the PS3 almost 2 years and let's see what it gives us. Remember folks, the PS3 isn't even out for a whole year yet and people are complaining. I don't think people realize that games take time to develop. Wii's games are limited to 1st party developers. The PS3 has a ton of developers who want to makes games for it. A good mix of 1st party developers and 3rd party developers such as Square-Enix of the Final Fantasy series and Konami - the Metal Gear Solid series will be set to appear on the PS3 as exclusives. The Wii will not be able to run those games even if they are ported because it is using dated technology. Those two games are two very good reasons to get the PS3.

Hardware and technology. The PS3 is built like a rock. It hardly breaks down compared to the 33% failure rate of the XBOX 360. Virtually no one has a problem with the PS3. It doesn't break cds, it doesn't give you the red ring of death, and it doesn't overheat. And as for the technology that is in the PS3 - you have a blu ray dvd player. Go out on the market and find on that is 499.99. You won't find one that is a better quality than what the PS3 has to offer. It's an above average Blu Ray dvd player. That says a lot considering that the blu ray players are way more expensive than the PS3 itself and they don't play games either. Built in WiFi for wireless internet connection which the Wii also has, but what the Wii doesn't have media sharing with PCs and MACs. With the PS3 you can play video, music, or even view photo albums found on your PC but on the TV using it's wireless connection. The Wii? It can only dream of doing that.

Conclusion - While the Wii offers a new way of playing games, it doesn't offer you anything else. With virtually no decent games for the Wii, it's 250.00 hassle. With the PS3 you are getting the best technology with next-gen graphics as well as a next-generation blu ray dvd player. Hence the price for 499.99. But it will be 499.99 well spent. The PS3 has exclusives that everyone is jealous about - Heavenly Sword, Lair, Soul Calibur 4 (the Wii doesn't get it, sorry guys), Devil May Cry, Metal Gear Solid 4, and Final Fantasy XIII. Why won't it be on the Wii? Because the Wii is sporting dated technology. Developers laugh at the Wii because of it's ability to display decent graphics. And with virtually no 3rd party developer support, you won't find much games for that system. 500 bucks is quite a lot for a console. But you will be getting the best of the best. With all the great technology and games, 299.99 is cheap.

Chapter 5

Voice and viewpoint in film reviews

Analysing a film review

Here are two examples of film reviews; the first one demonstrates how to be informative in a positive and entertaining way, whereas the second review reveals how you can use sarcasm and humour to criticise a film.

Quiz Show

Robert Redford's powerful statement on American ethics questions the truth of television in 50s America. Quiz Show is a true-life story of Twenty One, a highly successful game show in which the former contestants claimed the whole thing was rigged. It explores the American dream, where the ordinary man can make it to the top - in this case, it's Herbie Stempel (Turturro) who wins the hearts of the American public before being ousted by the all-American hero Charles Van Doren (Fiennes)

Not simply a study of quiz show corruption, the film is an indictment of American society, and outlines the phenomenal influence of television. Don't be put of by it two hours running time – with strong performances from Rob Morrow and Ralph Fiennes, the action moves swiftly. Both provocative and entertaining, Redford manages to create the mood of 50s America by intuitive directing and his subtle condemnation of American society.

Annotations:
- Use of adjectives
- Concise style
- Comment on social significance
- Personal opinion given in summary
- Direct appeal to the reader
- Sophisticated vocabulary

Chapter 5

Concise summary of the plot →

Wagons East

Its unfortunate that John Candy's last feature film does not live long in the memory. Set in the 1800s, this American Western comedy centers on Phil Taylor (Lewis), a nervous surgeon-cum cattle rancher, and his journey back to his native East. This predictable farce covers their treacherous journey east, which even involves meeting an Indian tribe – how original! It's perhaps an overstatement to describe this hapless movie as a comedy; with wooden performances and a tasteless script its PG rating should perhaps be changed to DG – Don't Go!

← **Use of sarcasm**

← **Adjective choice denotes meaning**

Use of humour →

Chapter 5

Film: Coraline

Reviews

- This dark edge will be the biggest test of the film as a commercial prospect: it may be too terrifying for the target audience. But for braver kids – and parents – this is a thrilling, even challenging ride.

- Technically, it's impeccable. But it's madly out of synch with the 12A certificate. Some scary fun.

- A gorgeously hand-crafted and pleasurably detailed piece of work. It's also genuinely strange, creepy and arresting.

- The results are simply astonishing. Selick has created a richly detailed, beautifully realised set of parallel worlds and allows us to become as lost as Coraline herself in and between their exquisite textures.

- Coraline is more of an odd curiosity than a must see, lacking the storytelling innovation to match its visual panache.

Chapter 5

Film: Hannah Montana

Reviews

- The film slips into American schmaltz at times, but it's really a thing of wonder — an infectious and irresistible fantasy that all the family can enjoy.

- You have to be true to yourself and your roots, particularly if you live a lie. As moral messages go, the one peddled by Hannah Montana the Movie could do with some fine-tuning.

- This parent-child love story, glancingly expressed through the potent medium of country music, often had me wondering if anyone in the cinema had a number for Tennessee social services.

- You might be rather surprised at just how likeable the bubblegum teen romance of Hannah Montana: The Movie actually is. And this is due in no small part to the superior comic acting chops of amiable bow-legged songbird, Miley Cyrus.

- A commercial product it may be, but there's a lot to like in this well-crafted Disney confection, which presents a positive role model who learns the value of family, friendship and the perils of losing that to fame and popularity.

- Fans will love this bright if bland romp, but it lacks that crossover appeal to make it it a guilty adult pleasure.

- Extolling the virtues of honesty, decency, friendship and family while portraying capitalism as the root of all evil, this big-screen outing for Disney's latest pop princess is a wholesome treat for her legions of young fans.

- With its kid-friendly mix of tunes and chaste romance, this is sure to leave its target demographic grinning widely.

- Kids will love this, put adults might find this a bit too much.

Chapter 5

How to write your own film review

The following list gives suggestions on how to write a successful film review. However, the key points are that it should be lively, entertaining and informative. Not all film reviews follow this format – it is important that you develop your own individual style when writing any type of review.

1. Title – catchy, can indicate if review will be positive or negative, you can play with words to make it funny or different (You may wish to do this after the review has been written)
2. Opening paragraph – can start to summarise film and give early suggestions about your general view of it (positive/negative). Provide brief details of the director, lead roles etc.
3. Provide some background information about the film. Dates/Location/Cost. Is there any interesting gossip or controversy surrounding the film?
4. Positive aspects about the film. What did you like? Why? Use descriptive words and think about the story, setting, effects used, music used.
5. Negative things you thought about the film. What didn't you like? Why? Comment on the same type of things that you mentioned in paragraphs 3 and 4. Was it perhaps unrealistic, sluggish, far fetched, over-sentimental or lacking in excitement?
6. Characterisation – Consider the characters carefully, especially the lead roles. What was it about their portrayal that you liked or didn't like? Other impressions of the characters, will certain audience members be able to relate to certain characters? How? Will certain audience members not like certain characters? Why not?
7. Comment on the purpose of the film. – To entertain, inform, excite, disturb, shock etc. Is the director trying to get across a certain message about society or the way people interact? Is there a political message? What is the intended affect on the audience? Explain whether you believe the film achieves its purpose.
8. Final comments – general comments that summarise your view of the film. Leave the reader with a sense of whether you recommend the film or not.

Challenge 23

Using the ideas discussed, produce your own film review on a movie you have seen recently. Remember it does not have to be positive, though you do need to justify your views and write in the appropriate style.

Writing a book review.

This can often be a daunting task, particularly when faced with a very complex and detailed plot to plough through. It is vitally important to communicate the moments of the book that appealed to you (or otherwise) rather than retell the plot and describe each character in depth – your reader will only want to get the essence of the story; remember also, you don't want to ruin the plot by revealing too much.

Chapter 5 — Challenge 24

Look through the following book reviews and consider how the opinions are expressed in a concise and informative way.

Book	Bootleg
Extracts from review	**Key elements**
The plot follows the story of a nightmarish future of banned sugar and chocolate, where the 'Good for You' party dominate and control the enjoyment of others. The story follows the struggles of two boys, Smudger and Huntley, as well as their able side-kick, Mrs. Bubby have in putting chocolate underground for the masses of people who are upset about the chocolate ban.	Concise description of plot, which focuses on the the charcater's journey, as well as the world that they live in.
I was not looking forward to this book whatsoever – the title/front over and blurb are very dull, uninspiring and very off-putting, especially when you consider the length. 345 pages about banned chocolate did not inspire me one bit. However, the style of writing is very subtle, engaging and instantly appealing to both children and adults alike. The subtle use of irony and the description of the characters' thoughts is humorous, heart warming and almost as addictive as the chocolate in Mrs. Bubby's shop.	Personal response, reveals expectations

Effective use of adjectives
Reference to who it might appeal to |
| It was fantastic to read something with a sense of irony, satire and escapism, rather than the usual collection of gritty, hard-hitting drama which is currently being released. You never take the action too seriously, and do have the sense that the world will still be ok by the end, yet the sense of childish adventure and sheer fantasy is awe inspiring at times. I particularly liked the stereotypical goodies and baddies, as well as the side-splitting touches of the nun who was locked up for the crime of eating chocolate. | Interesting comparisons and links made |
| On a deeper level, there are parallels with One Flew over the Cuckoo's Nest in a strange way – the indoctrination, coming back with no zest for life after bring re-educated. Also, the young upstart, Frankie, was suitably loathsome, until the interesting twist by the end. In addition, the relationship between adults and children is very well-developed, as are the family scenes. Even though Ron is in prison, the story never becomes too over sentimental or clichéd in presenting a dysfunctional family. | Examples from the book which highlight the level of interest

Gives examples of comparative books.

Explores themes and relationships between characters. |

Chapter 5

Book	Going Straight
Extracts from review	**Key elements**
The plot follows the physical and emotional journey of Luke, a dysfunctional teenager who manages to find a new lease of life through his involvement with Jodi – a blind girl who he becomes inadvertently entangled with through his failed attempt at stealing her father's trainers out his car. He is at the centre of the police struggle to get proof of the real car thieves, Mig and Lee – the stereotypical villains. As part of his punishment Luke agrees to meet the victims of his 'crime' and help out Jodi in her marathon training.	Plot focuses on the events as well as the characters' journey
Although the idea of a wayward teenager who finds solace and redemption in an unlikely source, is not an original idea, the sensitive and subtle relationship between the villain (Luke) and victim (Jodi) is created cleverly and without over-sentimentality. Her father's reaction is predictable yet his realisation by the end is touching, surprising and allows the reader to empathise well with Luke's situation.	Explores themes
There is much symbolism created, through the sense of running away from troubles – the failed attempt to steal the trainers could be used as a metaphor for Luke finally having to avoid running away from troubles and having to confront them. Similarly, Jodi's blindness is an interesting contrast to Luke's inability to 'see' the error of his ways, unlike Jodi. They draw strength from each other, and Jodi, especially, realises that she is running away from her own claustrophobic existence. There is another interesting contrast between the freedom that Luke exploits and abuses – he wants stability yet gets none; whereas Jodi's family are stable, reliable and supportive yet are unable to give Jodi the freedom and independence she craves. The two extremes in family relationships could be an interesting discussion and what makes a good family.	Explores imagery – use of symbolism

Analysis of characters' relationships |
| The dual plot of Jodi's run and Luke's predicament are interesting to the very end, especially when the two events are cleverly entwined on marathon day. All of the characters could be said to be running away from something, whether it be responsibility (Luke's parents) or letting go (Jodi's parents) Furthermore, the notion of facing up to your crime and meeting your victims is a very topical and relevant issue in the governments current theories on crime prevention. This could lead to much in way of the issues of crime and how best to deal with offenders. The book is an emotional journey symbolised cleverly through the well crafted dialogue, subtle use of imagery and the sense of anticipation maintained to the end. | Discusses style of book and its effect on the reader |

Chapter 5

Producing a critical review in an informed and articulate way.

When you read/see/play something that does not agree with you, and then are asked to write about it, it is very easy to be overly critical and lack sophistication in your writing. Effective reviews, even when they are damming about their subject matter, still need to communicate calmly, rather than simply scream at the reader. Look through the following review of The Summerhouse and consider how the style is critical though remains articulate in the way it is communicated.

Book	The Summer House
Extracts from review	Key elements
A very interesting idea which does not quite come off unfortunately. The story follows the literary adventures of a group of young people who have a childish fascination with a reclusive writer. This fascination becomes satisfied when they realise that not only is the polish man very 'un scary' he is actually a source of their admiration as they help to jointly produce a novel. Quite an old-fashioned tale in some respects, with some echoes of Enid Blyton in the sense of childish journeys.	Overview of disappointment
	Parallels with other novels
The idea of a story within a story is not original yet it is developed in greater depth in this novel, with much of the latter action following the fantasy fortunes of Luma and co in their fight against the GM baddies. I particularly liked the way that the writing process was explored – a huge help and possible inspiration for budding teenage writers; however, it was very far-fetched and unrealistic at times, with the teenagers coming up with one-word responses, which led miraculously to very pacey storylines. Moreover, writing is a very solitary and independent process and rarely stems from a collection of diverse views.	Some positive elements mentioned
Character wise, the old cliché of dysfunctional teenager (Charlie – living in a home/misunderstood/failing at school) finding escapisms and hope in an unlikely source, rears its predictable head again; as does the way that Abby uses the writing process as a way of helping her deal with personal grief of losing her sister. Very touching yes, but original, no. Also, the way that the prolific writer, Stan, an apparent recluse, amazingly allows these children into his house and takes on their advice, is also very romanticised and unlikely. I was hoping for a Boo Radley type situation (To kill a Mocking Bird), and they even steal the communication through posting notes idea, yet Stan's character is extremely under-developed, despite much intrigue and mystery created early on.	Explores the themes and questions how they were explored
	Begins to analyse the plot

Chapter 5

Book	The Summer House
Extracts from review	**Key elements**
As to the sub-plot, the science-fiction element is very uninspiring and lacks the type of character development needed to maintain reader interest. This story begins to dominate the whole action by the end, and the reader begins to feel quite diluted by the end and unsure where to put their priorities and interest. It therefore does not work because you don't quite know which story to become engaged in. Furthermore, the length of 350 pages is far too long to maintain the reader's patience, especially as there is so little mystery element. We always know there will be a happy ending in Stan's story and know that the book will be written and Abby and Choker will draw strength from the whole process. Overall, an excellent idea that doesn't quite work, mainly because of the uninspiring parallel narrative and wooden characters.	Tone becomes more critical though not a personal attack on the author. Respectful conclusion which includes some positives.

Challenge 25

Writing your own book review.

Choose a book (or short story/poem) and write your own review, using some of the techniques explored above. Your choice does not need to be a text you particularly like, though should be something that you have a strong view on (either positive or negative).

Chapter 5 — Challenge 26

Responding to controversy

In pairs, you need to discuss your responses to the following provocative statements
- War is great because all the bad guys get murdered
- People who eat meat are cruel
- Teachers deserve respect no matter what
- All teenagers should work at the weekends to pay for their education
- Stealing is ok as long as it's from a big company who wont miss it.

Future skills

You have been discussing school rules in the school council and the following list has been proposed. Produce an analysis of these rules for your headteacher and comment on whether they should be put in place.

Classroom Behaviour	Student Movement	School Dress Code
Students may not leave their seats or the classroom without permission.	Students will enter and exit the building by lining up at the place assigned to them, and will walk in and out in a quiet and orderly way.	Any form of dress and grooming that can be interpreted as a gang symbol is not allowed. (Example: boys wearing earrings known to designate gang membership.)
Disruptive behaviour, obscene or profane language, or defying teacher authority is not permitted.	Teachers will be present to supervise student movement into and out of the school. Individual students in the hallways are to walk quietly and are not to eat or drink.	Any form of dress or grooming that is clearly intended to insult someone or make them feel bad is not allowed. (Example: a T-shirt with something written on it that is disrespectful.)
Students are to eat only in designated school places.	Students in the halls during class time must have a pass from their teacher or the office.	Immodest dress is forbidden. This includes very short shirts for girls, or 'short shorts' for boys or girls, or very low necklines for girls.
Students are not to chew gum in class.	Students arriving late to school are to go directly to the security desk at the main entrance.	Students are expected to come to school clean. This means that they are washed, hair is combed, and clothing is neat and clean.
Students are not to wear hats or coats in class.		

Chapter 5

Personalised Progression

Assessment Focus 2 – produce texts which are appropriate to task, reader and purpose.

How is my work at KS3 assessed?

Your work is assessed using assessment focuses which help you and your teacher determine what level your work is currently at. This criteria is often used when assessing your APP work and other classroom assessments. In this unit we will be looking at how to progress in AF2 (see above)

Key questions:

- What level am I currently working at in this assessment focus for writing? (if unsure, ask your English teacher)
- What skills do I currently have in this assessment focus?
- What skills do I need to develop to get to the next level?

In this section, you will be completing a series of challenges which will show you how you can personally progress to the next level, using many of the skills that you have developed in this unit.

How can I practice my skills to reach the next level in this assessment focus?

In this assessment focus (AF2) if you are currently working at...

Level 3	**go to Progress Checker A (Level 3-4 progression)**
Level 4	**go to Progress Checker B (Level 4-5 progression)**
Level 5	**go to Progress Checker C (Level 5-6 progression)**
Level 6	**go to Progress Checker D (Level 6-7 progression)**

When you get to the stage where you feel that you are confident in a particular level in this assessment focus, you can attempt the challenges for the next level.

Chapter 5

Progress Checker A – (Level 3-4 writing progression)

	Assessment Focus 2 – produce texts which are appropriate to task, reader and purpose	
1	What level am I currently working at in AF2 writing?	Level 3
2	What skills do I currently have in this assessment focus?	As a Level 3 writer in AF2 I am able to: • make some attempts to establish purpose; • select some features of form to the reader • make some attempt to establish appropriate style.
3	What skills do I need to develop to reach the next level?	To be a confident AF2 writer at Level 4 I need to • make sure the main purpose of my writing is clear; • select the form of writing so that it is clear and appropriate to purpose; • use a style that is generally appropriate to task.

AF2 Progress Challenge
Moving a Level 3 response to Level 4

1) Below includes a Level 3 response in AF2. Look at how this pupil has achieved this level and think about what they could do to improve.

Task set: Your school is in danger of closing due to the number of parents who have decided to send their pupils to the new academy that has opened near by. Write a speech to parents in which you argue that your school is worth staying with.

AF2 – Level 3 response	**Why the pupils achieved a Level 3**
Hello everyone – I want to talk to you about ==our school== *and why it cant close. Its really important because it's a really good school and we* ==want you== *to still come here.*	• *Attempts to achieve purpose* • *Some appropriate features (use of adverb 'really' to express feelings)* • *Some appropriate style (persuasive comment ' we want you' – directly appeals to audience)*

Chapter 5

How could we move this response into Level 5?

AF2 – Level 3 response	**AF2 – Level 4 response**
Hello everyone – I want to talk to you about our school and why it cant close. Its really important because it's a really good school and we want you to still come here.	*I want to speak to you today to say how important it is that our school stays open. We know that you will help us so that pupils can still come here for years and years.*

Notice how the Level 4 response

- outlines its purpose;
- uses the correct (formal) tone;
- uses a persuasive style 'We know that you will'

Next steps…

1) Reread the last piece of writing you have completed and write down the following:
a) persona (what role have you been asked to take?)
b) audience (who are you aiming this writing at?)
c) content (what information have I used)
d) form and style (how should it be written (persuasively/descriptively/formally/informally)

2) Which aspects could you improve in order to make your writing move to a level 4 in AF2?

Chapter 5

Progress Checker B – (Level 4-5 writing progression)

\multicolumn{3}{l}{**Assessment Focus 2** – produce texts which are appropriate to task, reader and purpose}
1	What level am I currently working at in AF2 writing?	Level 4
2	What skills do I currently have in this assessment focus?	As a Level 4 writer in AF2 I am able to: • make sure the main purpose of my writing is clear; • select the form of writing so that it is clear and appropriate to purpose; • use a style that is generally appropriate to task
3	What skills do I need to develop to reach the next level?	To be a confident AF2 writer at Level 5 I need to • clearly and consistently maintain the purpose of my writing ; • clearly establish features of form which can be adapted to achieve purpose; • establish an appropriate style clearly to maintain reader's interest throughout.

AF2 Progress Challenge
Moving a Level 4 response to Level 5

The table below includes a Level 4 response in AF2. Look at how this pupil has achieved this level and think about what they could do to improve.

AF2 – Level 4 response	Why the pupils achieved a Level 4
I want to speak to you today to say how important it is that our school stays open. We know that you will help us so that pupils can still come here for years and years.	• *Clearly outlines purpose;* • *Uses the correct (formal) tone;* • *Uses persuasive style 'We know that you will'*

Chapter 5

How could we move this response into Level 5?

AF2 – Level 4 response	AF2 – Level 5 response
I want to speak to you today to say how important it is that our school stays open. We know that you will help us so that pupils can still come here for years and years.	Our school closing is unthinkable – it cannot happen. We need to work together so that our community appreciates what a good education we have been receiving for years and years. With your help, this horrible future can be avoided.

Notice how the Level 5 response

- is consistent in the way it tries to achieve its purpose;
- adapts writing style suitably using personalised language 'we' 'our';
- engages the audience through use of words such as 'community' to suggest shared ownership and responsibility;
- consistent tone used which helps persuasive intent.

Next steps…

- makes sure that every line of writing you produce has the intention of directly impacting on your target audience
- take on the role of your target audience and answer the following questions:

a) What would have an impact on me?
b) How could my mind be changed? (if a persuasive non-fiction text)
c) What would excite me? (if a descriptive text)
d) What would bore me and switch me off?

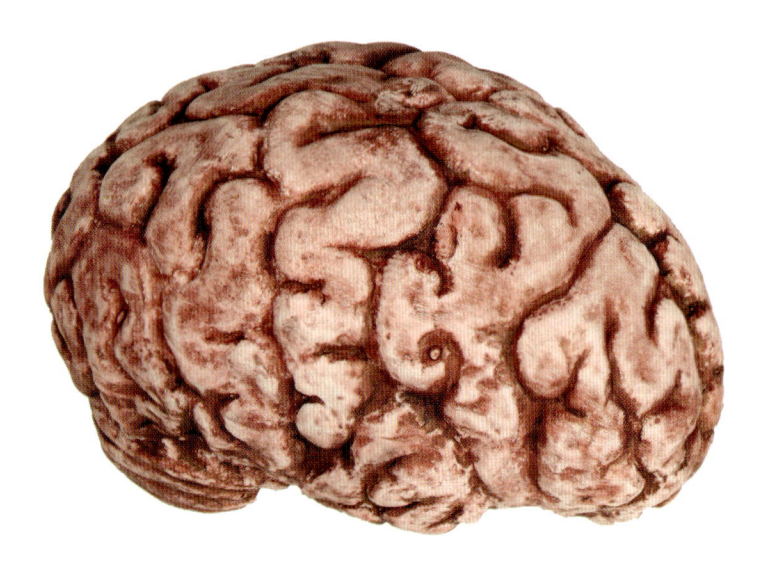

Chapter 5

Progress Checker C – (Level 5-6 writing progression)

	Assessment Focus 2 – produce texts which are appropriate to task, reader and purpose	
1	What level am I currently working at in AF2 writing?	Level 5
2	What skills do I currently have in this assessment focus?	As a Level 5 writer in AF2 I am able to: • clearly and consistently maintain the purpose of my writing ; • clearly establish features of form which can be adapted to achieve purpose • establish an appropriate style clearly to maintain reader's interest throughout.
3	What skills do I need to develop to reach the next level?	To be a confident AF2 writer at Level 6 I need to • imaginatively use appropriate materials and writing conventions; • adapt writing style to suit purpose and audience; • establish an individual voice or point of view that is mostly sustained throughout; • vary the level of formality used for purpose and audience; • use a range of stylistic devices used to achieve effects.

AF2 Progress Challenge
Moving a Level 5 response to Level 6

The table on the next page includes a Level 5 response in AF2. Look at how this pupil has achieved this level and think about what they could do to improve.

Chapter 5

AF2 – Level 5 response	Why the pupils achieved a Level 5
Our school closing is unthinkable – it cannot happen. We need to work together so that our community appreciates what a good education we have been receiving for years and years. With your help, this horrible future can be avoided.	• consistently tries to achieve its purpose • adapts writing style suitably using personalised language 'we' 'our' • engages the audience through use of words such as 'community' to suggest shared ownership and responsibility • consistent tone used which helps persuasive intent.

How could we move this response into Level 6?

AF2 – Level 5 response	AF2 – Level 6 response
Our school closing is unthinkable – it cannot happen. We need to work together so that our community appreciates what a good education we have been receiving for years and years. With your help, this horrible future can be avoided	*Can you remember the first time you came to our school? How excited your child was after their first day? A school isn't about shiny new buildings; it's about the people inside. That's why I love this place and why I want your support to keep it open.*

Notice how the Level 6 response

- imaginatively uses language to appeal to the audience
- adapts writing style to create a powerful impact
- establishes an individual voice which is personalised.
- varies level of formality to suit the occasion.

Next steps…

- Experiment with using different voices (personas) when producing writing
- Rate the impact of each statement you make – how could you increase this impact?
- Vary your formality, depending on the needs of your target audience

Chapter 5

Progress Checker D – (Level 6-7 writing progression)

	Assessment Focus 2 – produce texts which are appropriate to task, reader and purpose	
1	What level am I currently working at in AF2 writing?	Level 6
2	What skills do I currently have in this assessment focus?	As a Level 6 writer in AF2 I am able to: • imaginatively use appropriate materials and writing conventions; • adapt writing style to suit purpose and audience; • establish an individual voice or point of view that is mostly sustained throughout; • vary the level of formality used for purpose and audience; • use a range of stylistic devices used to achieve effects.
3	What skills do I need to develop to reach the next level?	To be a confident AF2 writer at Level 7 I need to • successful adapt of wide range of forms and conventions to suit a variety of purposes and audiences; • establish and sustain a distinctive individual voice or point of view; • control the level of formality and vary my use of stylistic devices to achieve intended effect.

AF2 Progress Challenge
Moving a Level 6 response to Level 7

The table over the page includes a Level 6 response in AF2. Look at how this pupil has achieved this level and think about what they could do to improve.

Chapter 5

AF2 – Level 6 response	Why the pupils achieved a Level 6
Can you remember the first time you came to our school? How excited your child was after their first day? A school isn't about shiny new buildings; it's about the people inside. That's why I love this place and why I want your support to keep it open.	<ul><li>imaginatively uses language to appeal to the audience</li><li>adapts writing style to create a powerful impact</li><li>establishes an individual voice which is personalised.</li><li>Varies level of formality to suit the occasion.</li></ul>

How could we move this response into Level 7?

AF2 – Level 6 response	AF2 – Level 7 response
Can you remember the first time you came to our school? How excited your child was after their first day? A school isn't about shiny new buildings; it's about the people inside. That's why I love this place and why I want your support to keep it open.	*I know many of you will have seen the brochures for the new academy, read the newspapers about how it's going to change education and turn us into geniuses overnight though some shiny, soulless building can't replace the warmth of our school, can't replace our school community which includes you as much as the pupils who have been so lucky to be educated here, to be looked after here, in good times and bad.*

Notice how the Level 7 response

- Recognises the needs and concerns of the target audience;
- Uses wide range of rhetorical features and emotive language to appeal to its target audience;
- Presents a distinctive voice which is passionate and respectful of the target audience.

Next steps...

- Use a variety of stylistic features when communicating to your target audience
- For each question/description you may use, respond as if you were your target audience.